A Brief History of World Slavery

What Happened,
Why it Happened,
and
What We Should Do About It

Glenn Rogers, Ph.D.

Simpson & Brook, Publishers
Abilene, Texas

Table of Contents

Introduction

I'm writing this in July and August of 2019 and already the rhetoric of the 2020 presidential campaign is hot and heavy. One of the topics that has come up in the past few presidential campaigns is the idea of reparations being paid to African Americans because their ancestors were enslaved. Already, several democratic candidates have said that reparations ought to be paid. They don't seem to have any formula or mechanism for how this ought to be done, but they are adamant that Africans are owed money for what happened to their ancestors. This strikes me as odd since African Americans are not the only ones whose ancestors suffered the indignity of slavery. Perhaps those who are advocating reparations are unaware of this historical fact. Perhaps they are also unaware that many (perhaps most) of the Africans who came to America as slaves were captured and sold to European slave traders by other Africans.

As I listen to people discuss the topic of slavery, it is apparent that there is a great deal of historical information that is missing in their view of things that happened in the past. It occurred to me that a brief volume on the subject might help shed some much needed light on the subject of slavery around the world from ancient times to the present.

In regards to slavery, people need to know what happened, why it happened, and how we ought to deal with the fact that it did. Are reparations appropriate? I don't see how singling out one group of people and paying them for something that happened to virtually every group of people, irrespective of race, could possibly be the appropriate thing to do. But that is my opinion. After you read this small book, you will need to make up your own mind about how to deal the with issue of slavery—past and present.

Chapter 1
Life Before Slavery

Early humans, from about 125,000 years ago to about 12,000 years ago, lived in nomadic bands, family groups of between ten and fifty people, who followed flocks and herds of animals as they moved about in search of water and grazing. Today we refer to those early humans as hunter-gatherers. The men hunted, providing meat for their small tribe; the women gathered fruits, vegetables, and grains. From archeological evidence, we know that these were large, powerful people—in part because of a protein rich diet that included lots of meat.

Nomadic Bands
Life was simple. You needed food, water, and shelter. Since most of their food traveled on four legs in search of grazing and water, the humans followed the animals. Where the animals went, the humans went. But in addition to food and water, those small tribal bands also needed friendly interaction with other nomadic bands. One reason for this

was the need for marriage partners for their children. Early on, humans figured out that too much inbreeding did not produce healthy humans. Marriage partners needed to come from different family lines. While they did not understand the science behind the need for genetic diversity, they understood the poor results of marriage partners from one's own close family. So they cultivated good relations with other family bands that hunted and gathered in nearby territories. However, it was also important for survival that not too many tribal bands tried to hunt and gather in the same areas. Hunter-gatherer bands were, therefore, somewhat territorial. And when a tribal band moved into the territory of another band, there could be conflicts. War. And when there was a conflict, the point was to kill the other people. The taking of prisoners (who might then become slaves) was not part of how they lived. People needed to be fed. Taking new people into your band meant that everyone's share of the food was a little smaller. Taking prisoners was a burden. So you killed your enemies.

Here's one of the things we have to understand about life in that time: at that time, humans as a species were very young, childlike in many ways. They had not yet figured out that killing is not a good thing. In time, that would become apparent. But it hadn't yet. So life was cheap, and there was a lot of killing. How should we think about that? We should understand that at this point along the trajectory of our human development we know that killing is not a good thing and we, except in certain extreme circumstances (self-defense, war, and so forth), do not condone it. But ancient people had not yet figured that out. So we need to cut them some slack. They didn't understand. When a baby messes its diaper we do not think it evil or inhuman. It's a baby. Messing its diaper is what it does. As it grows and develops, it will stop messing its pants. Allegorically, ancient humans were a lot like children. There was a lot they didn't understand, so they did things that we, in our time, know are wrong. We understand; they didn't. Let's give them a break.

For most of the time humans have populated planet earth, slavery did not exist. But life was cheap. If someone who was not part of your family or tribal band became a threat or a problem, and you couldn't convince him to go away, you killed him. This was the way life was for many thousands of years. It was to everyone's advantage to keep to themselves and mind their own business, being careful not to encroach on someone else's territory.

Settled Villages

Since the women did the gathering in those early millennia of human existence, they were the one's who noticed how vegetables and grains grew. As they moved from place to place over the seasons of a year, they noticed how a few seeds left behind this time around would generate new plants (vegetables and grains) next year when they passed that way again. It may have even been the case that they began intentionally leaving seeds so that next time they passed that way there would be more food to gather. In other words, they began experimenting with dry farming— horticulture. Eventually, they figured out how to cultivate plants of different kinds, which meant that they could grow food intentionally instead of being limited to finding things growing wild. That was a life-altering discovery.

At some point, the women of the tribal band explained this to the men of the band, pointing out that constantly being on the move wasn't necessary because they could grow food instead of having to go out and hunt for it. They could grow the kinds of fruits and vegetables and grains that grew in a given geographic region, making constant travel unnecessary. Traveling all the time was hard on the young and old people of the group, so there was an advantage in settling down and staying in one place.

While it is impossible to know how the men of the tribe, the hunters, reacted initially to this suggestion, we know that eventually, even if it took years or generations to make it happen, it did happen. One by one, tribal bands began travelling less and staying longer in one place, building shelters of one kind or another to live in. Villages began to spring up in places where there was water nearby, and fertile land where grain and vegetables could be grown. The men would still go hunt, perhaps being gone for many days at a time, but would bring the meat back to the village.

While the women were doing the farming, the men, when not hunting, were experimenting with domesticating goats and sheep. They domesticated and trained dogs to help herd the flocks they began to develop. Eventually, they did not need to go hunting, because they had sheep and goats that could provide the meat their family needed.

The first place all of this domestic activity began was in the fertile plain between the Tigris and Euphrates Rives in the Middle East in the ancient region known as Mesopotamia, now known as Iraq.

Technological Progress

We normally think of technology as things like computers, cell phones, scientific equipment, and so forth, and do not, therefore, think of the ancient world as having much in the way of technology. But figuring out how to get water from the river to the field to water crops was a technological advance. In fact, learning how to irrigate a field was the single most important technological advance of the ancient world. It made it possible to grow more food, to feed more people. But it also meant that there was a lot more work to do.

A Change in Perspective

As more crops were grown and bigger flocks and herds were kept, the need for more people to do the work increased. And since raids and war parties remained part of ancient life, it occurred to someone that instead of killing one's enemies, capturing them and bringing them back as slaves who could be forced to work was a good way to get the additional labor one needed. Thus, the birth of slavery.

As far as we know, slavery began about 10,000 years ago in the Middle East in the first ancient civilization known as Sumer (Meltzer, 1993:9). According to Kramer, slavery soon became a recognized institution (1963:78), with most of the slaves being gathered in raids against neighboring villages, towns, or cities. That means that race was not an issue in slavery. If the slaves were from neighboring villages, towns, or cities, the people taken in raids were not of a different race. They were not people from a distant land. They were Sumerians. Sumerians enslaved Sumerians. If you were the victor in a conflict, you captured people who would

11

serve as your slaves. If you were the loser in a conflict, you became a slave. The stronger ruled the weaker. The stronger oppressed the weaker. If you were strong enough to be the victor in a conflict, you were able to force the conquered to serve you.

What we will see in this brief study of the history of conflict and slavery is that *every group of people at one time or another were in the unfortunate position of having been the defeated. Every group of people out there, on every inhabited continent, were at one time or another, defeated by another, stronger group of people and were made to serve that stronger group of people.* The servitude had nothing to do with race, color, language, culture, or other differentiating factors. It was simply a matter of having been defeated by a stronger group of people. If you were part of the conquered, you became someone's slave. You were his property, had no rights, and did as you were told—or suffered severe consequences (Kramer 1993:78).

How should we think about this ancient change of perspective that allowed one group of people to enslave another? We should understand that their thinking was a product of their time and place. This is not to say that their thinking in regard to slavery was right. But it was what everyone in the world at that time thought. Slavery, like killing, was simply part of the way life was lived at that time. Doesn't make it right, but it was the way those people thought and behaved.

Again, do we condemn a child for being a child? No. We understand that the child does not yet understand and will, in time, grow out of his childish thinking and behavior. If, when he is twenty-three, he is still behaving as if he were three, there is a problem that needs to be addressed. But when he is three, his behavior is normal for a three-year-old. So let it go. Give him a pass. This is what we must do with ancient people who did not yet understand that slavery was not a good thing.

Summary

As far as we know, slavery did not exist during the time of the hunter-gatherers. During that time, humans lived and traveled about in small family or tribal bands and hunted and gathered the food they needed to live on. Only after settled village life began and food production began did the idea of capturing and keeping slaves to do the hard work occur to anyone.

The slavery that was practiced at that time had nothing to do with the race of the slave. Slaves came from nearby villages and were not of a different race. Sumerians enslaved Sumerians from different villages. In fact, slavery has never had much to do with race. It has always been about labor and economics.

How should we think about slavery in the ancient world? While we do not want to appear to condone the oppression and enslavement of any group of people, we must understand that at that time, slavery was simply part of how life worked. If you were part of a stronger people, you conquered and enslaved people. If you were part of a weaker group of people, you were oppressed and enslaved. It was not right, but it was how things were at that time. Today, we think differently about slavery. We consider it wrong. The ancients did not. They were wrong. But ancient humans were very much in a childhood phase of human development and just didn't know any better. So, just as we excuse the behavior of a three-year-old, let's give the ancients a pass on things they did not yet understand.

Chapter 2
Slavery In the Ancient World

We have established that slavery likely began about 10,000 years ago, not long after people began living in settled villages. Nearly as soon as people began forming those small societies in ancient Mesopotamia, the people from one village began fighting with those of rival villages. Wars, big or small, have dominated human history. We are a violent race. Sometimes a dispute between two groups might arise over territory—water or grazing rights. Sometimes the impetus may have been a personal grudge. Sometimes, no doubt, it was merely a desire to dominate. But whatever the reason for the fight, those who survived the conflict were taken captive and made to serve those who defeated them.

A few examples will demonstrate the pervasiveness of slavery in the ancient world. These are not the only places slavery existed, but serve merely as examples of how slavery existed throughout the ancient world.

Sumer

When people lived as hunter-gatherers, the men were hunters; the women were gatherers. Men had the skills of hunters; women had the skills of gatherers. But when people began to live in settled villages, over time people began to develop new, specialized skills. If a village was near either the Tigress or Euphrates Rivers, some men might have decided to become fishermen. Others may have chosen to focus their energies on building herds of goats and sheep. Yet others may have decided to focus on growing grain. Some became masons, learning how to make sunbaked mud bricks and how to use those bricks to build houses. Some concentrated on religious rituals and became the first priests. Others worked with leather to make sandals, belts, bags, and so forth. Some helped to develop a written language and became scribes and teachers.

Along with the development of labor specialization, came the need for social norms and laws. When different families came together to form a village, all they had were their individual family traditions and customs for how to live. But multiple family groups living together in close proximity in a village required that there be some agreed upon rules. The village elders would have gotten together and come up with some agreed upon rules—what we would call social norms. These village rules or laws were the first legal codes to be formed. Eventually, they would be written down.

One of the best known ancient legal codes of the ancient world is the Babylonian Code of Hammurabi, which we will discuss in regards to slavery in a few moments. In addition to legal codes, villages that grew into larger social complexes also developed formal religious institutions that included a temple and a priesthood. Ancient societies also developed economies, which at first were likely barter systems, but then morphed into a basic system of capitalistic free enterprise (Rogers 2018). Along with these basic features of a fully formed society—social norms, a legal code, formal religion, and an economy—came social stratification (Woolf 2005:69).

Social stratification in the ancient world was exactly like social stratification in our modern world. Social stratification is not the result of a planned attempt to create a stratified society. None of the village elders or city councilmen or mayors or kings or whatever they called themselves ever set out to create a stratified society. No one came to a meeting and said, *Hey, guys, I got an idea. Let's create a stratified society.* Social stratification is the inevitable, natural, and automatic result of labor specialization and social complexity. Some jobs are just more important than others. For instance, the priests, who were thought to have the ear of the local god, were important people. What they said carried a lot of weight. The king or other city officials, regardless of title, were more important than a guy who sold the fish he had caught. Scribes and teachers held positions of high social rank, as did successful business people. Some career choices generate more income than others. That was true then just as it is now. The guy who sold grain that could be ground and made into bread probably made more money than the guy who sold sandals. Why? Because wives needed to make bread several times each week. Therefore, they bought a lot of grain. People don't buy sandals as often as they buy grain for making bread. The people who made more money had a higher social standing. Why? Because they were considered more powerful, more influential. Today, sociologists identify three things—wealth, prestige, and power—as the basis for social stratification. It was the same in ancient times. The people who had the wealth, the prestige, or the power occupied the higher social strata. As noted, this is the normal, inevitable outcome of social growth and complexity, which includes labor specialization. There was nothing wrong with it in ancient times, and there is nothing wrong with it today.

Babylonia

On top of the social pyramids of the ancient world were priests and kings. On the bottom were slaves. The Code of Hammurabi made it clear that slaves were not considered people, but merely property (Leick 2003:39). Their owners could do with them as they could with any of their other property—utilize them any way they wished. What was it like to be a slave in ancient Babylonia under those conditions?

While slaves had virtually no standing as people, they were considered a valuable asset, not only to his or her specific master, but to the society as a whole. A healthy slave was a productive slave. Therefore, the law sought to protect the lives and economic value of slaves. Masters could not simply kill their slaves, and if a slave was injured by someone, his master had to be compensated (Meltzer 1993:16). In some cases, a slave enjoyed a measure of freedom, depending on the specific job he did for his master. Some slaves were able to engage in business and even own slaves of their own. This, however, was not typical, and slavery in any form is still slavery. When you belong to another, even if your job is not horrible, your life is seriously diminished. And for every slave that worked in a household and lived a semi-normal life, there were many others who worked difficult jobs in the fields or some other kind of difficult physical labor.

While most slaves were captured in raids on neighboring villages or cities, some were born into a household, and some sold themselves or their family (or members of their family) into slavery to pay off debts. Many slaves were purchased. Ancient Babylon had a thriving slave market (Roberts 2002:97).

What kind of work did they do? Some slaves worked in the fields or cared for flocks and herds, some were household slaves whose jobs involved cleaning, fetching, serving, and possibly sex. Some owners treated their slaves better than others. In some cases, on a day-to-day basis, depending on the kind of slave one was (a household slave for instance), one's life might not be very different from a poor but free person of the city. The free person, however, was free. The slave was someone's property. Slavery was never a pretty thing.

Egypt
Egypt is one of the oldest civilizations in the world. Not quite as old as Sumer, but close. The Egypt civilization, like all ancient civilizations, included slavery, though it was apparently less important in Egypt than in other Middle Eastern cultures (Roberts 2004:122). Many slaves in Egypt served in various capacities in the temples rather than with private citizens because the average private citizen in Egypt lived very humbly as peasants (Meltzer 1993:29).

Apparently, quite a number of Egypt's slaves were captured in military campaigns (Wilson 1951:271), though not all were. The ancient Hebrews (the biblical *Children of Israel*) provide an example of an entire group of people who were pressed into slavery while living within the borders of Egypt.

Slaves who served in the temple complexes would have had jobs more like household slaves—cleaner and easier. But those who served in ways similar to the Hebrews—making bricks, hard physical labor outdoors— would have known daily drudgery and suffering.

Israel

The Hebrews, also known as the Children of Israel, were the descendants of Abraham, a man from the Mesopotamian city of Ur who was, as the biblical story goes, called by God to go to a distant land that would be given to his descendants. Abraham obeyed God, making the perilous journey to Canaan, where he settled. His son Isaac had two sons, Jacob and Esau. Jacob had twelve sons, one of which was Joseph. In a rather sad story of a family torn by jealously, Joseph ends up being sold into slavery in Egypt. However, in an amazing turn of events where God was with Joseph, protecting and watching over him, Joseph becomes Viceroy in Egypt, second in power only to Pharaoh himself. When a famine hits Canaan, Joseph is in a position to help his family, even though they had treated him so horribly. Eventually, Jacob's family of seventy people move to Egypt where there is food, and Joseph is able to offer them a comfortable life. It is an inspiring story of divine providence and forgiveness.

However, after the Pharaoh and Joseph both die, the new Pharaoh is not friendly toward Joseph's family that is growing at an alarming rate. Abraham's descendants, by then known as Hebrews, are pressed into service of the state—slavery—with the specific responsibility of making bricks to be used in building Egyptian cities. It was hard, hot, dirty work. For four hundred years, they served as slaves in Egypt, growing into a nation of several million people during that time.

When God decided that the Israelites, a people he had created for a special purpose, had been in slavery long enough, he raised up a leader, Moses, to free them. The story of the Israelite exodus from Egypt is told in the Bible, in the Old Testament book of Exodus.

After a contentious departure from Egypt, the Israelites camped at the foot of Mt. Sinai where Moses went up the mountain and received from God the Ten Commandments and 603 other laws that would serve as the legal code for the ancient Hebrew theocracy. Among those laws were regulations for how slaves were to be treated—with justice, kindness, and consideration. Specifically, the law of Moses (as it was called) forbade kidnapping or capturing a person and making him or her a slave. Second, slaves were to be treated with kindness and compassion. And, when a slave was freed, he or she was to be given a generous portion of supplies so he would not be destitute. Finally, there existed in the Law of Moses a celebration called the Year of Jubilee. Every fifty years, in addition to other considerations, debts were to be forgiven and all slaves were to be freed.

Those were excellent laws that made slavery in ancient Israel less ugly than it was in other cultures. Still, one has to ask, why did God allow slavery under any

21

circumstances? Why didn't he just forbid it? He forbade murder, adultery, bearing false witness against your neighbor, coveting, and so many other things. Why not just forbid slavery? Good question. The best answer I can come up with is that in some cases, slavery was designed to protect a person from the liabilities associated with debt. If one got into debt and could not get out, one could sell himself into slavery where he could work off the debt. During this time, instead of being destitute or worse, thrown into debtor's prison, one could serve in a household, having food and shelter, until such a time that his debt was satisfied. It was a kind of social welfare system.

The other reason that God did not simply forbid slavery, I believe, was that it was simply part of the fabric of the ancient world. Every culture made use of slaves. It was simply part of the way the world worked. I do not believe that God approved of it any more than he approved of wars, violence, oppression, and patriarchy. But those things were part of human life at that time, and until humans grew and developed to the point of deciding for themselves that such things were not part of how people ought to live, God was willing to tolerate such behavior. Like the parent who tolerates childish behavior from their three year old, God tolerated childish behavior from ancient people.

Some, no doubt, will object saying that slavery is not simply childish behavior, but immoral, degrading, hurtful behavior. Yes, that is one way of looking at it. I'm not sure that is how God sees it, but then his perspective is quite superior to ours.

To complicate matters even more, God did not condemn slavery in the New Testament. Why not? Because it was such a huge part of the first century world, of the Roman Empire. Condemning slavery outright would have been useless. God did, however, require Christians who owned slaves to treat them with kindness and consideration.

Whether my answers to the question of slavery in both the Old and New Testaments are sufficient is for others to decide. Perhaps instead of trying to figure out why God did what he did, our time would be better spent is remembering that slavery was pervasive in the ancient world. Every culture utilized slavery, and it had nothing to do with race. It was purely an economic concern.

Greece

The Greeks, possibly the most enlightened culture of the ancient world made extensive use of slaves in their society. In fact, their culture was predicated on the use of slaves (Woolf 2005:319). It is estimated that in many Greek cities slaves represented perhaps 30 percent of the population (Freeman 1996:172). How could that have been the case among such enlightened people? How did thinkers like Plato and Aristotle justify slavery?

Plato's thoughts regarding non-Greek people reflected those of the Greeks in general. For the Greeks, people who were not Greek, who did not speak Greek, were barbarians. They were unworthy of freedom. They were a step beneath the Greeks, and as such it was appropriate that they serve those who were above them. The color of the non-Greek person was not a consideration. The mere fact that they were not Greek was enough to identify them as unworthy of freedom. Is this racism? If racism is the idea that one group of people is superior to another (and that's what racism is), then yes, it is racism. The ancient Greeks, who thought themselves superior, were racists. Oddly, though, their "racism" had nothing to do with one's race or ethnicity—the color of one's skin. Most of their slaves would have been other white people from cultures surrounding Greece. It simply did not matter what color one was or where one's ancestors had come from. If you were not Greek, you were a barbarian, and were, therefore, inferior.

That most of the slaves in ancient Greece were other white people does not mean there were no black slaves. There were. The Egyptians routinely made trips to the south and brought back captives from Ethiopia so serve them (Thomas 1997:27). Some of those slaves were sold and shipped to Greece. But it would be a mistake to assume that their slaves were all black Africans. They were not. Most were other European people the Greeks had conquered. Why? Because it simply did not matter to them what one's race was. If you were of a conquered people, you were a slave.

Aristotle, Plato's student, took a different approach in his justification of slavery. Aristotle argued that some people were simply not capable of rational thought and therefore not able to be fully responsible people. He believed that some people were born to be slaves, needing someone to do their thinking for them, to give them work they were capable of doing.

I am a philosopher and hold Plato and Aristotle in very high esteem. However, on the point of slavery, they were simply wrong. Each was a product of his time and place and had to form opinions about human nature, value, and intelligence without the benefit of modern research and knowledge. Like the rest of the world at that time, the Greeks believed slavery to be a legitimate feature of social life.

There were probably more female slaves in Greece than male slaves. Most of the men who went to war against the Greeks were killed. So most of those brought back after a conflict were women and children. Meltzer notes that:

> Women slaves did not work on the farm. They did the chores of the master's household. They washed, spun, wove, cooked the meals and served them, prepared the bath, and attended the bed chambers. If they were young and pretty, they went to the master's bed. That was the custom throughout Greek history (1993:48).

While most of the slaves in Greece were women (Camp and Fisher 2002:45), there were still a good number of male slaves, many of which eventually served in a *polis*-owned and managed corps of police whose job it was to maintain order in assembly meetings (Cartledge 2002:110). Imagine a citizen, with all his feelings of superiority, becoming unruly at a city assembly and having a slave, perhaps who was just learning to speak Greek, confront him about his behavior. Awkward.

Greek slaves, like slaves in other cultures could be freed or could earn or purchase his or her freedom. And some did, becoming wealthy slave-owners themselves. How could one who had been a slave become a slave-owner? Seems rather hypocritical. Not from the perspective of an ancient person. Remember, slavery was considered normal and moral. There was no reason a slave or a former slave could not own slaves.

The Greeks had many admirable traits. They gave us philosophy and democracy. Much of our Western worldview and culture is rooted in the philosophical soil of ancient Greece. But when it came to slavery, they bought into the idea just as thoroughly as every other culture. As enlightened as they were, the Greeks had not yet realized that one group of people ought not to oppress and enslave another. Indeed, it would be nearly 2,500 years later before Western cultures finally eliminated the practice. So it wasn't just the Greeks who were at fault, it was everyone.

Rome

For much of its history, Rome was a slave society on a massive scale, and servitude did much to corrupt and coarsen Roman life. Although the institution went back to early times, only the very rich could afford to keep slaves in the first centuries of the republic. Everything changed with the wars of conquest of the second century BCE, after which hundreds of thousands of foreign captives were sold into slavery in Italy, 150,000 alone after Rome's victory against the Macedonians at Pydna in 168 BCE. To compound the problem, pirates based on Crete and the Turkish coast roamed the eastern Mediterranean snatching victims for the slave

market on the Aegean island of Delos, which
was said to be able to handle 10,000
transactions a day. Many of these
unfortunates also found their way to Italy
(Woolf 2005:379).

A rough estimate is that in the first century BCE
there were between 1.5 and 2 million slaves in Italy (Beard
2015:329). That's a lot of slaves, and they engaged in a wide
variety of activities. Some slaves worked in agricultural
contexts doing farm work. Others, in contrast, were highly
educated and trained professionals such as doctors, architects,
and teachers (Adkins and Adkins 1994:342).

As an example of the kinds of slaves a person of
wealth and influence might have, Beard recounts the slave
staff of Cicero, a Roman statesman who served as consul in
63 BCE. Records show that he had "... just over twenty
slaves: a group of six or seven message boys, a few
secretaries, clerks, and 'readers' (who read books or
documents aloud for the convenience of their master), as
well as an attendant, a workman, a cook, a maidservant and
an accountant or two," (2015:328). Scheidel offers a more
expansive list, noting that "slaves were engaged in an
enormous variety of activities, as estate managers, field
hands, shepherds, hunters, domestic servants, craftsmen,
construction workers, retailers, miners, clerks, teachers,
doctors, midwives, wetnurses, textile workers, potters, and
entertainers (Scheidel 2012:90).

How a slave was treated and what kind of life he or
she lived depended greatly on the job he or she had. For
instance, slaves who worked in the fields (which would have

been men) were often chained together as they worked and at night were locked away as prisoners (Adkins and Adkins 1994:342), while those working as teachers, doctors, business managers, and so forth may have lived in sometimes luxurious surroundings in their master's home. Some were treated cruelly; some were treated graciously, to the point of being paid wages, which allowed them eventually to buy their freedom, eventually becoming wealthy in their own right (Adkins and Adkins 1994:342).

Despite the lavish contexts in which some slaves lived, the legal reality was that slaves in Rome lived at the bottom of the social structure and had no rights whatsoever (Meltzer 1993:176). They were property to be bought, sold, and utilized however their owner saw fit: beat him, kill him or send him to his death in the arena. Slaves had no legal right to get married. If a slave woman gave birth, her child was the property of her master. And while many masters were kind to their slaves (a healthy, happy slave was a productive slave) the mere fact of being a thing rather than a person was demoralizing and depressing even for slaves who were otherwise treated well. I have heard people claim that African slaves who were brought to America were treated worse than any slaves in history. That is simply not true. Slavery in every culture, with the possible exception of ancient Israel, was ugly, demeaning, and dehumanizing.

One last point about Roman slavery—it had nothing to do with the color of one's skin or where one's ancestors had come from. Google a map of the Roman Empire. It was a Mediterranean empire. The people they fought and captured (which is where most of their slaves came from) were Mediterranean people, many of whom looked very much like and had cultures very much like the Italians. Roman slavery was not rooted in racism; it was rooted in imperialism. If your people were conquered, and if you survived your encounter with the Roman legions, you became a slave. If you were lucky, and if you had a valuable skill, you might live out the rest of your life in a tolerable context, but you would do so knowing that you had no rights and could be disposed of at any time for any reason. Being a slave in ancient Rome was no picnic.

However, as in ancient Greece, there were black African slaves in Rome. They probably came from Ethiopia by way of Egypt (Thomas 1997:27). But they were there. They were in the minority, but there were black slaves in ancient Rome. Most of the slaves, however, were not African, but from the regions at the borders of the empire.

Slavery in Other Ancient Cultures

So far we have highlighted slavery in some of the cultures known better to historians who focus on Western history. But slavery was a worldwide phenomenon. Slavery existed in ancient China, Japan, and other Asian cultures, in India, and in Mesoamerica (the Aztecs and Mayans). Native Americans engaged in slavery, capturing peoples of neighboring tribes, utilizing them in forced labor. African tribes did this same thing, raiding other nearby tribes, taking prisoners, making them slaves. Africans enslaved Africans. Europeans enslaved Europeans. Middle Eastern people enslaved other Middle Eastern people. Asians enslaved Asians. Every cultural group that was strong enough to attack and defeat another group of people incorporated slavery into their social framework at some time during their history. Most of them did this for thousands of years. The strong would oppress and enslave the weak. Then, as time passed, the weak would become strong and turn the tables on their oppressors, enslaving them. For example, the Greeks enslaved the peoples they defeated, but eventually they were defeated and became slaves themselves.

War and slavery were fundamental characteristics of the ancient world. It wasn't right, but it was the way things were. There is no point in ignoring slavery or denying it. History is what it is. It cannot be changed. The thing to do is understand that while lots of bad stuff happened in centuries past, lots of good stuff happened as well. And isn't that the way life still works? There is lots of bad stuff going on in the world today. But there is lots of good stuff going on as well. The human reality is a blend of good and bad. We hope that most of the time the good outweighs the bad. It doesn't always, but we should always be working toward that goal.

Here is an interesting question to think about. If you could trace your family line back far enough, would you find that your ancestors were slaves or slaves owners? It might be that at some time your ancestors were slaves, and at other times they were slave owners. What has that got to do with you? Are you a slave? Are you a slave owner? You are probably neither a slave nor a slave owner, and are unlikely to ever be either. So why does what happened to your ancestors matter? In the ancient world, slavery was a reality. What has that got to do with how you live your life? If one of your ancestors 9,000 years ago was a slave owner, what has that got to do with you? Nothing. If one of your ancestors 9,000 years ago was a slave, what has that got to do with you? Nothing. It might be an interesting piece of historical information, but it has nothing to do with who you are and how you live your life.

Summary

As soon as humans began living together in formed societies, they began fighting with neighboring settlements over various concerns—everything from territorial rights, to personal grudges, to the simple desire to dominate other people. As soon as this kind of fighting began, slavery began. People on the losing end of the struggle were taken captive and forced to serve those who had defeated them.

Slavery was everywhere in the ancient world: Sumer, Egypt, Israel, Greece, Rome. But slavery was not only found in those cultures, it existed the world over. There was slavery in China, Japan, and other Asian cultures, in India, and in Mesoamerica. Native Americans enslaved each other, as did Africans. Slavery was everywhere. And it was not based on enslaving people of other races. People from one city in ancient Mesopotamia would enslave people from other cities in Mesopotamia. Ancient slavery had nothing to do with race or color. It was a simple matter of strength and economics. The strong oppressed the weak because they could, and because it was economically beneficial.

Slavery was pervasive in the ancient world, and it may be that one of your ancestors was a slave owner. Or it may be that one of your ancestors was a slave. What has either of those things got to do with the person you are today? Nothing.

Chapter 3
Slavery in the West from the
Fall of Rome to the Industrial Revolution

When Rome fell, much of Western civilization crumbled to the ground. Oddly enough, slavery was one of the social constructs that survived. Another was Christianity. As they had for almost 500 years at that time, those two institutions would continue their uneasy alliance for another 1,300 years.

Western Society After the Fall of Rome

Politically, socially, culturally, and economically, Rome had served as the West's focal point for centuries … Millions of people from the lowest reaches of the Danube River to the windswept hills of northern Britain built their lives around Roman power and authority. Suddenly, in 410, that power and authority could no longer be depended upon (Davenport 2007:11).

As the Visigoth king, Alaric, moved from Roman city to Roman city, laying waste to the empire's centers of economic activity, the frightened and shocked citizens who survived the ordeal (and most did) began to focus their hope for something approaching a normal life on the rural estates that were often bypassed by the invaders. Many of the country estates included land holdings large enough to produce a sizable crop. People were drawn to these estates, looking to the Lord of the manor as a source of security. Where there was land to be worked, food could be grown and life could be lived, even as the once glorious Roman Empire crumbled to the ground.

As the formal empire continued to crumble, the rural estates grew in importance. The estate owners became the guardians and benefactors of the people who lived and worked their land. Previously, in the days of the Empire, one could be wealthy without owning land. But as the European economy shifted away from money as wealth to land as wealth, the landowners became powerful and important people in the new social order that was developing. The Catholic church also served as a stabilizing factor, assuring the people that God would work things out.

Even though many of the people who looked to the estates for their livelihoods were free people, there were still vast numbers of slaves who also worked the land. Who were these slaves? They were the people or the descendants of people who had been conquered by Rome. That is, they were Europeans. White people. White people enslaving white people; Europeans enslaving Europeans. It had nothing to do with race, ethnicity, or the color of one's skin. These were the people who had been part of the Roman Empire who were now part of the social shambles left in the wake of the Visigoths' destructive rampage. The slaves who served on the country estates after the fall of Rome may have been some of my or some of your ancestors. We will probably never know for sure, but depending on where your ancestors lived, it is certainly possible.

The migration (or invasion—depending on your point of view) of the Vikings into England in the late 700s did not change much in relation to slavery. When the Vikings arrived in England and along the European coast, they (for the most part) overwhelmed the local peoples and took captives. But soon after the violence of their arrival ended, they became traders and merchants. They had little use for slaves, so they sold many of them in Constantinople or Spain.

As time passed and the Dark Ages (the period following closely upon the fall of Rome) became the Middle Ages, the social structure known as Feudalism enveloped Europe. Social distinctions tended to be less strict. The lines between slave and serf (nearly a slave, but not quite) and between serf and free but poor people were not always clear (Meltzer 1993:209-210). Warfare continued as the king of one region would attempt to expand his holdings and power by going to war with a neighboring king. As had been the practice for thousands of years, the victor would take captives from the conquered people who would then serve their conquerors as slaves. It was not a racial concern; it was a power concern. If you were strong enough to dominate another people, they became your servants. So the practice of

34

Europeans enslaving Europeans continued. The slave trade was a vibrant business, and "until the Normans conquered the country [England] in 1066, many Englishmen were sold abroad in the slave markets of Europe and the East. William the Conqueror (1066-1087) permitted domestic slavery to continue, but he banned the sale of English slaves overseas" (Meltzer 1993: 210).

My ancestors on my father's side were English. And they were certainly not wealthy. Maybe one of my ancestors was one of those unfortunate Englishmen who lived and died as a slave.

The Church and Slavery

Where was the church during all this time? Why weren't they denouncing slavery? Good question. As mentioned earlier, God had allowed the practice of slavery in the Old Testament Law of Moses. Why had he done that? I believe that the wrongness of slavery was one of the things that God knew people needed to figure out for themselves. God had condemned bearing false witness against one's neighbor, murder, adultery, and a host of other practices that he labeled as sinful. But he had not labeled slavery as sinful. Neither had he labeled patriarchy (the male domination of home and society) as sinful. Why not? Surely, God did not intend for males to consider women as inferior, dominating them at every turn. Surely, God did not intend for one group of people to oppress and dominate another group of people, forcing them to serve as slaves. I agree that God did not intend for men to dominate women or one group of people to dominate another. So why did he not condemn either patriarchy or slavery? Because as I said earlier, God

35

understood that the lessons one learns best are the lessons one learns for him or herself. God knew that humans would grow out of patriarchy and slavery. He knew that we would eventually figure out that one person oppressing another or one group of people oppressing another is not good and that we ought to give up that sort of behavior. And for the most part, we have.

Perhaps you can make that argument in relation to the Old Testament law, a more primitive law for a more primitive time and a more primitive people, but surely in the New Testament, a more enlightened approach to human interaction, God would have chosen to condemn slavery. One might think so, but he did not. Through his apostle, Paul (Ephesians 6), God required slave owners to treat their slaves with kindness and consideration, but he did not condemn the practice.

So in a world—the world of the Middle Ages—where slavery was still alive and well, the church did not condemn slavery. The church does not make up rules (at least it's not supposed to), it simply teaches and explains the rules God has set forth in scripture. So, since God did not condemn slavery, the church did not condemn slavery—at least not in any wholesale fashion, proclaiming that slavery was utterly sinful and must be stopped. There were, however, isolated attempts by various church leaders and some monarchs to curb the practice, especially the enslaving and selling of Christians. Generally speaking, however, slavery continued to be an accepted practice.

Surely allowing slavery to continue was a mistake on God's part. Really? We're going to judge and condemn God now? Actually God is the one who does the judging and the condemning. God knew that in time humans would figure out that slavery is wrong. And as I said in an earlier chapter, for the most part, we have, and have condemned it. Why do I say for the most part? Because unfortunately, in some very dark places in the world, forms of slavery still exist. We shall discuss that before we complete our study, but for now it is enough to say that for the most part human beings have come to see that slavery is wrong. That was not the case, however, in the Middle Ages or the ages to follow in that dim and difficult time in the development of Western civilization.

The Life of a Slave in the Middle Ages
A bishop named Alfric who lived in the late 10th century wrote about slavery. In his writings he included a slave's account of his workday.

> I go out at dawn driving the oxen to the field and yoke them to the plough. It is never so harsh a winter that I dare lurk at home for fear of my master, but when the oxen have been yoked and the ploughshare and coulter fastened to the plough, I must plough each day a full acre or more … I must fill the oxen's manger with hay, and water them, and clear out the dung … It is heavy work because I am not free (Meltzer 1993: 213).

This account has to do with the field preparation and subsequent planting of the field. On the other end of the process, of course, was the harvesting aspect of farming:

Bringing in the crop, threshing, grinding, or otherwise processing it, and making it available for distribution.

Slaves also served as blacksmiths, brickmasons, carpenters, shepherds, cooks, cleaners, household servants, personal assistants, doctors, teachers, oarsmen, sailors, soldiers, and more. Any job that needed doing, a slave might be asked (if qualified) to do. They were considered, as slaves had always been considered, as property with a standing equal to that of cattle. They could be dealt with as their master saw fit. A slave in the Middle Ages lived essentially as slaves had lived 8,000 years before in the ancient Middle East.

While many of the slaves in the Middle Ages were war captives, many were not. Sometimes people sold themselves into slavery because of debt. Sometimes parents sold children into slavery because they couldn't afford to keep them. Sometimes people were put into slavery as a punishment for a crime.

Slavery, in what the West refers to as the Middle Ages, was not confined to Europe. Slavery, between 500 and 1800, existed pretty much as it always had throughout the world. After the fall of Rome and into the modern era, slavery existed in the British Isles, the Byzantine Empire, the countries that participated in the Crusades (maybe you want to Google that), the Middle East, throughout the Ottoman Empire, in Poland, Russia, and Scandinavia. During those years, there was also slavery in China and other Asian countries, and in Mesoamerica, and in North America among Native Americans. In other words, slavery existed pretty much everywhere.

The trading of slaves flourished in a number of major economic centers, including a number of cities in Italy. Constantinople and Genoa carried on a significant slave trade, as did various centers in Spain. Slavery was still considered completely acceptable by just about everyone, and existed virtually everywhere.

Christians Enslaved by Muslims

Since few have actually studied the history of slavery, most people are unaware that for hundreds of years vast numbers of Christians were enslaved by Muslims. To be fair, though, it must be pointed out that during the Crusades many Muslims were enslaved by Christians. But there was a unique situation that developed between 1500 and 1800 where the enslaving of white European Christians by Muslims was a thriving business. Muslims, like every other group of people, simply assumed slavery to be a fact of life (Thomas 1997:37). In his book, *Christian Slaves, Muslim Masters: White Slavery in the Mediterranean, the Barbary Coast, and Italy, 1500-1800*, Robert C. Davis tells the story of this little known piece of history.

Even among those familiar with the history of slavery, there has been little work done on the Mediterranean slavery of white Europeans. Why has this been the case? One reason is that many historians are more interested in researching and writing about the injustices perpetrated by white people on non-white people than those perpetrated on white people. In other words, the trend in university history departments has been to focus on the bad things white people did but to ignore the bad things that were done to white people.

Another reason there has been little work done in the area of the Mediterranean slave trade is that it was assumed that the numbers of whites enslaved were small and the impact of this activity negligible. However, the work of Davis and a few others have demonstrated that this is not the case.

How did this Mediterranean slave trade work? Basically it was the work of Barbary Coast pirates who captured ships, taking the crew and passengers captive and selling them as slaves.

The Barbary Coast was the coastal regions of North Africa. The modern countries of Morocco, Algeria, Tunisia, and Libya are the countries that would have been known as the Barbary Coast between 1500 and 1800. How large was this slavery enterprise? Davies notes that:

> Diplomatic reports, popular broadsheets, and simple word of mouth circulated throughout Europe, telling and retelling of Christians taken by the hundreds of thousands on the high seas or during coastal sorties, and hauled off in chains to a living death of hard labor in Morocco, Algiers, Tunis, or Tripoli (2003:5).

After presenting quite a bit of interesting data regarding Christian slaves in Muslim hands, Davis boils it down to a number that demonstrates that Barbary pirating was no small-scale enterprise. He says, "The result, then, is that between 1530 and 1780 there were almost certainly a million and quite possibly as many as a million and a quarter

40

white, European Christians enslaved by the Muslims of the Barbary Coast" (2003:23).

In comparison to the 10 to 12 million African slaves brought to America during those years the number seems small. But a million or a million and a quarter people being taken as slaves is not insignificant, and the impact ought not to be minimized. On an individual basis, the suffering of each of those million or more white people was just as great as the suffering of each of the 10 or 12 million black people brought to America.

Slavery is a bad thing. It doesn't matter who is taken as a slave, being treated as less than a human of equal standing is horrible, and all who suffered such indecency suffered in ways God did not intend. No one should be subjected to the horrors of slavery. But many people were. Over the centuries, as many white people suffered as slaves as did black people. Did the color of their skin increase or lessen the depth of their suffering?

Summary

The fall of Rome threw Western society into a tailspin. As city after city fell to the Visigoths, people who survived their encounters with the barbarians were drawn to the country estates where there was a way to grow food and care for one's family. The estate owners became lords who, along with the church, brought order and security to daily life. And while a new social structure (Feudalism) would develop and function in Europe for a few hundred years, slavery continued to be a reality, making the darkness of the Dark Ages even darker for some.

The Catholic church was one of the most important stabilizing factors after the fall of Rome. Why didn't the church oppose slavery? Because God had seen fit to let humans decide about the rightness or wrongness of slavery for themselves, and humans, as a group, had not yet come to the realization that slavery was an ugly dehumanizing institution. Why would God leave something like that up to humans? I suspect because he understood that the lessons people learn best are the ones they learn for themselves. By letting humans come to their own realization about the wrongness of slavery, he was allowing them to learn an important lesson that they would value forever.

What was it like to be a slave in the Dark and Middle Ages? It was awful. It was the same horrible experience it had been 8,000 years before. The institution of slavery didn't become more civilized with the passage of time. Slaves were considered property, like cattle, or sheep, or donkeys, or dogs. Masters could do with their slaves as they wished. And even if you were one of the lucky few who served as a household slave, living in a nice house, doing cleaner, less difficult work, the very fact that you were not free made your life a drudgery. But most slaves were not household slaves. Most worked in the fields or the mines, doing difficult work for long hours. Slavery being what it was, the life of a slave was ugly and hopeless.

One of the lesser known episodes of slavery had to do with Christians being enslaved by Muslims. Between 1500 and 1800, from a million to a million and a quarter white European Christians were taken as slaves to serve in Muslim societies. Most were taken by Barbary pirates, whose ships roamed the Mediterranean looking for

42

unprotected ships to attack. And while the one to one and a quarter million Christians who were taken and made to serve Muslim masters is considerably less than the 10 to 12 million Africans who were taken to America to be slaves, we must consider how being a slave impacted each individual. Clearly, each of the one to one and a quarter million white slaves suffered just as much as each of the 10 to 12 million black slaves, for slavery is horrid regardless of the color of the slave.

Chapter 4
The African Slave Trade

Just as the people in the region of ancient Mesopotamia had been enslaving each other since the beginning of civilization, so too, Africans had been enslaving other Africans since ancient times (Meltzer 1993:Book 2:17). As the Greeks and Romans enslaved the captives they took in battle (which were usually neighboring peoples of the same race), so too, one African tribe would go to war with another, and the conquering tribe would enslave the surviving members of the other tribe. When they did not need the slaves for their own purposes, they sold them to Arab traders, who, in turn, sold them to other interested parties. So really, the African slave trade began long before the Europeans came on the scene, with black Africans enslaving and selling black Africans.

Early European Slave Trading

The European slave trade began in the year 1441, when a little Portuguese ship commanded by young Antam Goncalvez captured 12 blacks in a raid on the Atlantic coast of Africa. The prisoners were carried back to Lisbon as gifts for Prince Henry the Navigator (1394-1460). Delighted with his new slaves, Prince Henry sent word to the Pope, seeking his approval for more raids. The Pope's reply granted, "to all of those who shall be engaged in the said war, complete forgiveness of all their sins." In 1455 a papal bull authorized Portugal to reduce to servitude all heathen peoples (Meltzer 1993:Bk2:1).

Historical facts do not attempt to sugarcoat the truth. For anyone who claimed to be a Christian, especially one who claimed to be the leader of the Christian church, such an attitude and such an action is utterly stupid and shameful. But then human beings often behave in stupid and shameful ways.

So there it is, the Catholic church and the Portuguese collaborating in what became the beginning of the European slave trade of African peoples. But before we get carried away with our criticism of them, remember that at that time slavery had been an accepted behavior for thousands of years, and black Africans had been capturing other black Africans and selling them as slaves for millennia. So let's not demonize the Europeans as if they were behaving beyond the norm.

Africans Selling Africans

Within a dozen years of the Goncalvez voyage, the small and sporadic slaving raids on the African coast gave way to organized trading. The Berber chieftains of the southern Sahara traded horses for slaves with the black rulers, usually getting 10 or 15 men for a horse... The slaves in turn were sold by the Arabs to the Portuguese... By 1552 Lisbon's slaves numbered 10,000—in a population of 100,000. There were more than 60 slave markets in the city... In the fifteenth century the slave trade extended all through eastern Africa. Swahili agents handled it for Arabs, who shipped the blacks to Arabia, Persia, and India in their own dhows... The Swahili traders worked with the tribes just off the coast, who raided farther inland for captives (Meltzer 1993:Bk2:2-3).

Before the Europeans arrived, the slaving in Africa was likely on a smaller scale, though as noted, thousands of black Africans were sold to Arab traders. However, as the need for slave labor rose in Europe and later in America, African tribes realized that there was money to be made. Lots of money. So the number of raiding parties and their frequency increased. The costal tribes would send raiding parties inland a hundred and fifty miles or so to capture people to be sold to the European traders. Many, perhaps most, of the slaves eventually came from what is now referred to as sub-Saharan West Africa, with the majority, many believe, coming from the inland regions between Ghana and Nigeria.

My point in this brief section is that the African people were complicit with the Europeans in the enslavement and transport of between 10 and 12 million Africans to serve as slaves in the Americas, many of them in the southern regions of the United States. This is not conjecture; it is historical fact. In Calibar, Cameroon, a city I have visited a number of times while living in southeast Nigeria, there is a slave museum built on the site of the actual slave market that existed there in the seventeen and eighteen hundreds. The museum displays various artifacts used in the trade and tells the story of the slave trade in that location.

I am not intending in any way to excuse the role of the Europeans in the slave trade. Still, it must be acknowledged that they were only one participant in an activity that involved multiple participants. I remember when the movie version of Alex Haley's *Roots* came out in 1977. Lots of people watched and were horrified as European slavers raided a village and captured a number of people to transport to America. The problem with that presentation is that it left people with the impression that all the slaves were captured in such a manner. This, as we have seen, is simply not the case. Very few Europeans raided villages to capture black Africans to take to Europe or America. They bought people who had already been captured by other Africans. So let's not vilify the Europeans as if they were responsible for the entire ugly process. They were not. They were one party engaging in a business that had been a business for nearly 10,000 years. Does that make it right? No, of course not. But let's not pretend that it was white men doing bad stuff to black people. Black people were part of the process. For thousands of years, white people had enslaved other white people, and black people had enslaved other black people. At one time or another, just about everybody oppressed and enslaved somebody else. Let's tell the story accurately, as it really happened.

The Perilous Transatlantic Passage

Getting the slaves from Africa to America was no simple task. Since the entire venture was about making money, the more slaves a captain could squeeze into the hold beneath the deck, the better. The trip took two months or more, and conditions were horrible.

> ...[S]laves were wedged into ship holds like logs and chained together... The space allotted for a male adult slave was not as large as a grave—5 1/2 feet in length, 16 inches in width, and 2 or 3 feet in height. Sometimes the height between slaves decks was only 18 inches. Often the slaves slept sitting up or on their sides, fitted together spoon fashion. They were let up on deck a few minutes a day for fresh air and exercise. To keep them in better shape, they were made to jump in their chains... If the weather was bad, they stayed

below. The holds were dark, filthy, slimy, and they stank; the food often spoiled, and the water became stagnant (Meltzer 1993 Bk2:46).

Because of the horrid conditions onboard the ships, sickness was a constant concern—for both slaves and crew. The slaves were packed in so tightly that often they could not move around enough to utilize whatever toilet facilities were available. Often they had to lie in their own waste. If they became seasick and vomited, they had to lie in that as well. It was hot below deck, and the air was foul. Many slaves ended up with dysentery, which only made the problems worse. Scurvy and small pox were also problems, as was syphilis, since crewmembers often raped the women slaves.

Because there was so much sickness, there was also a lot of death. If too many people became sick, it was possible that the illness would spread to everyone onboard, slaves and crew alike. Captains often had to remove the sick from the ship. Of course, the only way to do that was to throw them overboard. One captain reports having had to throw 135 slaves overboard during one passage (Meltzer 1993 Bk2:48). Mortality rates were often between 10 and 20 percent. It is likely that over a million slaves died at sea over the years during the passage to America.

The crew was impacted by sickness as well. The crew may not have been packed in as tightly as the slaves, but everyone lived in close proximity to each other. If sickness hit a number of slaves, the crew was at risk for contamination. Sick crewmembers were just as much of a threat to the successful completion of the undertaking as were sick slaves.

Additionally, there was always the possibility of a slave revolt. Even though they were chained, when they were brought up on deck for exercise, they outnumbered the crew. There are records of revolts where the slaves took over the ship, killing the crew and captain. It did not happen often, but often enough so that crews had to be alert to the possibility. The threat of revolt may have caused the crew to treat the slaves more harshly than would have been necessary, which in turn made the slaves all the more likely to attempt an uprising.

To say the journey was difficult is a considerable understatement. It wasn't just difficult; it was horrible. And it wasn't horrible for only the slaves. It was horrible for the crew as well. Everyone involved was forever tainted by the evil of the enterprise.

By the time it was all said and done, 10 to 12 million Africans had been brought to the Americas as slaves. The economy of the southern states was based on the labor provided by the slaves who came to the United States. It should never have happened. But the thing to remember is that the enslavement of Africans was only one chapter—a recent one—in an ages old story that began in antiquity. How many millions of slaves suffered and died long before the first black slave was brought to the shores of America? Many millions. They suffered and died just as many Africans suffered and died. Let's keep things in proper perspective. It is shameful that anyone was ever enslaved. But they were. The suffering of African slaves was no worse than that which had been endured by millions before them. Any time anyone is oppressed and enslaved, it is a horrible evil.

Summary

African slavery began long before the Europeans came on the scene. African tribes had been going to war with other African tribes, capturing men, women, and children to serve as slaves for thousands of years. When they did not need additional slaves themselves, they sold them to Arab traders. The age old practice of slavery existed worldwide. Africans practiced it just like everyone else.

The earliest European slave traders were apparently Portuguese. In 1441, Antam Goncalves raided a village and captured 12 people, whom he took back to Portugal as a gift to Prince Henry the Navigator. Henry, then, with the permission of the pope, undertook more raids to capture African people to serve as slaves. From that small beginning the practice grew exponentially, with the small village raids by Europeans giving way to a more practical and effective methodology: buying slaves from the stronger coastal tribes who trekked inland to capture people from the smaller, weaker inland villages. Slave markets where Europeans bought slaves from African slave traders made the whole process much simpler. In Calibar, Cameroon, a slave trade museum has been set up on the actual site of a slave market, serving as a reminder of how Africans were complicit in the sale of African slaves to Europeans.

Once the Europeans bought the slaves they wanted, they had to transport them across the Atlantic to somewhere in the Americas. To say that it was a difficult journey is a considerable understatement. The two-month long journey was a hellish experience for both slaves and crew. There was overcrowding, sickness, and death. Captains often lost between 10 and 20 percent of their "cargo" due to sickness.

Crew members also got sick and died. Occasionally there was a revolt where the slaves attempted to take over the ship. Sometimes, though not often, they were successful.

In the end, 10 to 12 million African slaves were transported to the Americas. It is horrible that such a thing ever happened. But it had been happening for nearly 10,000 years. Over the millennia that had passed since the beginning of civilization, many millions of people were captured and made to serve as slaves. Most lived and worked in horrible conditions. Africans were not the first, and unfortunately they will not be the last. For anyone who was ever enslaved, it was a horrible experience. It is shameful that anyone ever had to endure it.

Chapter 5
Slavery Should Never Have Happened …
Why Did It

Why did slavery ever happen? The short answer is because humans, in their early stages of development, didn't know any better. But that short answer may not be very helpful or meaningful, so in this chapter I will offer a longer, more detailed explanation of why one group of humans would oppress and enslave another group of humans. It is not my intention to excuse bad behavior, but rather to explain it.

The Fundamental Human Condition
The fundamental human condition is one of ignorance and narcissism in pursuit of understanding and growth. What does that mean? To adequately explain what I mean will require that I discuss a number of other things that might at first appear to be unrelated to the topic at hand. I assure you they are not unrelated, but lay at the very heart of the problem.

God—The Eternally Existing Rational Mind

To answer the question about why slavery ever happened, we must take a close look at the kind of beings humans are. To do that, we must delve into the origins of the human species. Who and what are we? Where did we come from?

Since I am a theist, I believe in God and the idea presented in the Bible that God created humans in his image. You may not share that particular belief, and that is fine. But for me to discuss why slavery happened, I have to start at what I believe is the beginning of the story.

As a philosopher, I define God as the eternally existing rational mind. That means that God is that which has always existed, and is who is responsible for everything else that exists, including humans, who, like God, are rational, conscious, self-determined beings. It is not my intention to "prove" anything here. I have offered logically sound proofs of God's existence in another of my books—*Proof of God*. If you are interested in that kind of material, the book is cited in the Works Cited section. For my purposes here, we will assume that the existence of God is not in question, and that he is the creator of all that exists. But to make my point it is necessary to discuss God's being and nature.

God is not a physical being, not an embodied being. He has no form of any kind. God is the eternally existing rational mind. Because he is not embodied, he does not exist in any one place, but exists in all places simultaneously. Because he is supremely rational, he is fully self-aware, and as a self-aware, rational, mind, he is self-determined.

For some reason, God decided to exercise his creative powers and create the universe, which involved creating the time-space continuum. Before God created it, there was no time and no space. There was just the eternally existing mind. But once God created the universe, time and space came into existence. God then decided to populate the universe with galaxies and solar systems. From the available evidence, it is apparent that he used what we refer to as the big bang to do so.

The planet earth was specially designed to support the development of highly evolved human life, so God began the evolutionary process to populate the earth with life. The process began with simple life forms that evolved, in some fashion, to more complex life forms. That's where the process became really interesting.

God Created Humans in His Image— Rational Minds

In the Bible, God tells us that he decided to create humans *in his image*. That means that whatever kind of a being God is, we are like him. Since God is a rational mind, we are also rational minds. We are embodied while God is not, but that is only a minor detail. The important point is that our essence is that of a thinking being. We are minds who happened to be embodied. Part of having a body means that we have a brain. The brain serves as the control center of the physical body. But we are not essentially a body controlled by a brain; we are essentially a mind—a thinking being, like God is a thinking being.

What process God used to create us in his image is not entirely clear. The story in Genesis Two about the mound of dirt should probably not be taken literally. It is an ancient story meant to satisfy the childlike minds of ancient people.

But whatever mechanism God used to create humans in his image makes us unique—completely different from animals. Because we are rational, we are highly aware. We are aware that we are aware, which makes it possible to think about abstract concepts in relationship to ourselves—rights, equality, justice, mercy, freedom, morality, the nature of the reality of which we are a part, and so forth. We can run *what if* scenarios, asking ourselves what we would do in this or that situation. Animals cannot do that. God can. And so can humans who are created in his image.

The problem of being created in God's image is that while the features and the nature are there, it takes time to grow into them, to be capable of using the abilities we have.

Baby Minds Struggling to Grow and Understand

When human babies are born, they have the potential to learn and understand many things. But they start off as something of a blank page and day by day learn about their environment, about life, about relationships and so forth. It takes years for babies to learn enough to be functional, so they can live in the world and participate in society. In some respects the brain develops quickly. But in some respects the brain develops slowly. The ability to think in the abstract, for instance, does not develop until around 11 or 12 years of age. What does this mean? It means that children cannot think about abstract ideas such as morality when they are six or seven years old. All they know is that Mom or Dad has told them that a thing (lying, for instance) is wrong. So they know that lying is wrong but cannot think about the concept of truth and untruth, and why the one is better than the other.

That ability doesn't come until later. Minds (and brains) must have time to develop their full capabilities.

If we understand how this works with a human child, we can understand how this same idea might work with humans as a species. When God created humans, he did not create them as fully intellectually mature beings. The first humans were very childlike, needing to learn and grow into the species they were capable of becoming. They were physically mature, capable of reproduction, but early humans (baby minds) needed time (many thousands of years) to develop their full analytical thinking abilities.

If you've had a course in Introduction to Psychology, you know the basics of human development. Babies and children are capable of certain things at certain ages. The six year old can do things the three year old cannot do. The fourteen year old can do things the six year old cannot. As the child grows and matures, so do the child's abilities. And one of those abilities is the ability to engage one's higher analytical thinking skills. The fourteen year old can think about morality in ways the six year old cannot.

What does any of this have to do with slavery? Be patient. We're coming to that.

The Developmental Trajectory of Humankind

The development of humanity is very much like the development of the individual human being. Do a Google search on *Erikson's 8 stages of psychosocial development*. It is an excellent model of how a human changes and grows as he or she matures moving from one stage of development to the next.

What I am suggesting is that humankind as a species is going through a similar developmental process as it matures, moving from one stage to the next. In ancient times, humanity was (intellectually speaking) in its infancy stage. From infancy, it moved to early childhood, from early childhood it moved to later childhood, then into adolescence. Late childhood to early adolescence in a human child is when mind and brain development is adequate to allow for abstract reasoning. In a similar way, when humankind was in its infancy, early childhood and later childhood stages, it had not yet developed the ability to think effectively about abstract concepts—such as morality, equality, personhood, freedom, self-determination and so forth. And it is these things, things that belong to the realm of abstract concepts, that are required for people to figure out that slavery is immoral.

So while humankind was in its infancy, early childhood, and late childhood, it was incapable of thinking about the kinds of things that would lead it to condemn slavery.

No doubt, someone will object that some of the greatest thinkers of the ages lived in ancient Greece, a time I am identifying as part of humanity's early childhood. This is true. And while the Classical Greek thinkers were advanced beyond their time in many ways, in many other ways they were products of their time and place. Both Plato and Aristotle failed to understand that all human beings were equal and had the same worth and value as every other human being, regardless of their cultural and linguistic differences. Very smart children, even gifted children, are still just children.

One of the reasons slavery happened is that humankind in those ancient times simply did not understand that what they were doing was wrong.

But what about later in history, the late Middle Ages or the beginning of the modern period? Surely by then people were developed enough to know slavery was wrong. That is assuming that during the late Middle Ages or the beginning of the modern period that humanity had developed into the adolescent stage where analytical thinking skills had developed sufficiently so the morality of slavery could be analyzed. I suggest that by the beginning of the modern period humankind was still in the late childhood stage and incapable of serious moral thinking.

Humans were very clever and learning a lot—scientifically speaking—but that is not the same as serious moral contemplation. Think about it, discussions about equality, freedom, self-determination, social structures, self-governance, and the morality of slavery came much later in history. Why? Because humanity was not yet ready to identify and discuss those kinds of subjects. Those kinds of discussions didn't really occur in any meaningful way (that is, they had not yet become part of public discourse) until the late 1600s and into the 1700s. When those kinds of subjects began to be discussed, slavery was one of them, and serious questions about the morality of slavery became part of public discourse.

So one reason slavery happened was simple immaturity. Another related cause was narcissism. Babies are supremely narcissistic. All they think about and care about is themselves—what they want, when they want it. If you are tired or asleep, they do not care. They will scream until you come and give them what they want. As they get older, they exhibit their extreme self-interest in not wanting to share their toys, in wanting only specific things to eat, and in being less than honest about all sorts of things. Babies and children are self-absorbed, and one of the more serious challenges parents face is teaching their children to be less self-centered and more considerate of others. It takes years for them to learn to do that. Some never learn. They live their entire lives as self-absorbed shallow people.

Ancient humanity, in its infancy and childhood stages, was very much like a narcissistic child, concerned only with what they wanted. If they were strong enough to take something from someone else, they took it. If they were strong enough to force someone into submission, they did so. If they wanted to make another person serve them, and were strong enough to do so, they did. Whether doing so was right or wrong did not occur to them. The narcissistic person doesn't question whether or not their thinking or behavior is correct. They simply assume it is and proceed with what they wish. And that's what ancient people did. Their cognitive development hadn't yet reached the point where they were capable of even thinking about personhood, equality, rights, freedom, morality, and so forth. And, like the children they were, they only cared about what they wanted. So, if they wanted a slave, they went out and got themselves a slave, never bothering to question the rightness of it, or to consider the needs and feelings of the other person.

Should slavery ever have happened? Of course not. But if we consider the developmental stage of early humanity, their ignorance, immaturity, and narcissistic tendencies, we can understand why they behaved as they did.

Fortunately, as humankind moved into what might be compared to the stage of adolescent development, they began to ask serious questions about the nature of life, including the rightness and wrongness of slavery. It took a long time for people to resolve the question in their minds. And not everyone agreed that slavery was wrong. Economic considerations, no doubt, muddied the moral waters. Here in America, it took a war to settle the issue. But at least the issue was settled. And over the next century, most people came to understand the wrongness of slavery, the wrongness of considering any person as worth less than any other person.

Many good things happened in the ancient world. People tried to figure out how to live together. Laws were written. Things were invented: the wheel, sunbaked bricks, the plough, irrigation systems, systems of writing. Civilizations were built. Ancient human beings were good people doing lots of good things. They just did not yet understand that in some ways they were behaving badly in how they interacted with each other. The thing to remember is that the bad behavior was not limited to any one group of ancient people, and the suffering caused by slavery was not limited to any one group of people. All ancient peoples engaged in slavery. At one time or another, just about every group of people who lived were either slaves or masters. The masters at one time in history may be the slaves at another. What goes around comes around. It wasn't that they were inherently evil people; they just didn't understand. As humanity matured and developed, they realized that slavery was wrong and adjusted their behavior—for the most part. Unfortunately, in some places, slavery still exists.

We Are Just Beginning to Understand

We humans think of ourselves as a fully formed, mature species. We are exploring the depths of the sea and reaching into space beyond our solar system. We are on the verge of curing cancer. Look at what we know; look at what we can do. Surely we are a mature, sophisticated species who is poised on the brink of greatness. Not so. Humanity, I believe, is still in its adolescent developmental period. That's why we arrogantly believe we are so advanced when in reality, as a species, we are just a silly, arrogant teenagers ... metaphorically speaking.

We have millennia of growth and development ahead of us before we really begin to understand, before we come even close to achieving our potential as a people. We have come far. No doubt about it. But we have even farther to go.

Summary

Why did human beings oppress and enslave one another? Because they didn't understand that to do so was immoral. God created humans in his image, which means humans are rational. highly aware, self-determined beings. But he did not create humans as fully mature beings who knew and understood everything they needed to know and understand. The first humans were childlike in that they needed to learn and grow into the mature species they were capable of becoming. Humankind had to develop in much the same way the individual human has to develop. Children do not develop the ability to think in the abstract, that is, to think about concepts such as rights, equality, freedom, justice, morality and so forth, until they are 11 or 12 years old, until they are becoming an adolescent. And even then, it may take several years before they actually begin to think about those things.

Generally speaking, humankind, on a developmental trajectory similar to that of a human individual, did not reach the developmental stage where it could think about important conceptual questions until the mid-1600s. That is when questions such as equality, self- governance, and the morality of slavery entered the public discourse. So the reason slavery existed was simply that humans were not yet capable of discerning that such behavior was wrong. That, along with the narcissistic behavior that is normal for children, made behaviors such as slavery nearly inevitable. Should it have happened? No. But it did because of the immaturity of humankind.

And it was not just one group of people who were guilty of that bad behavior. All peoples were guilty of it. Every group of people made use of slaves.

It would be nice to be able to say that slavery is a thing of the past, that humanity had finally ridded itself of that horrid evil. But we cannot. Slavery still exists. We shall discuss that concern in Chapter 7.

Chapter 6
Was America's Economy Built
on the Backs of the Slaves

You often hear that America's economy was built of the backs of the slaves. Is that true? No. It is absolutely not true. People who make such statements betray their ignorance of what a national economy is—of what it consists, and how it works. Or, if the misinformation is not the result of ignorance, it is the result of a far left, Marxist agenda driven presentation of history. That is, a slanted, dishonest presentation designed to promote a liberal, Marxist point of view. If I had to choose between the two, I would rather the inaccurate comment be rooted in ignorance. But either way, America's economy was not built on the backs of slave labor.

Inaccurate Conclusions
Those who make the mistaken claim that slave labor was the foundation upon which the American economy was built will often reference the fact that for a period of time in the mid 1800s cotton was the United States' chief export.

From that single fact, they conclude that the entire American economy was based on slave labor. But that is simply not the case, and a closer look at the various components of the economy of the United States in the 1700s and 1800s will make that clear.

Family Farms

Not everyone who came from England or Europe to America was wealthy enough to own slaves. Most of the poorer families who came here survived by working small family farms, growing just enough to meet their own needs. They did not own slaves or utilize slave labor. Even after the beginning of the industrial revolution in America (1790), most of America's population consisted of farmers. And most farms were small family farms. Most of the slaves in America were found on the larger plantations in the south. But there were millions of small family farms in America operated without slaves. The people who pushed westward, opening up the frontier in search of land did so without slaves. For instance, my ancestors on my mother's side came from Germany and the Netherlands. Early on, they migrated to Tennessee, and from there made their way to Kentucky. According to my mother, my grandfather's grandfather was part of the group that traveled from Tennessee with Daniel Boone, establishing Boonesborough, Kentucky. They were not wealthy people who owned slaves. As most people who moved West in search of land, they were poor farmers.

Most of the slaves were owned by plantation owners in the South. Look at a map. The southern states where slavery thrived do not even make up 25% of the continental United States. As the western frontier was opened up and family farms (or ranches or other family endeavors) were established, African slaves were virtually unknown. And it was these pioneers who established not only farms and mills, but who built towns with stores, and churches, and schools. In a very basic way, those were the people who built America and its thriving, multifaceted economy. What were some of the elements of that young economy that developed without a contribution from slaves?

Early Economic Enterprises

Three early economic enterprises that were major features of the developing American economy were fishing, shipbuilding, and the fur trade.

Because of the poor quality of the rocky soil in New England, many who settled along the northeastern coast turned to fishing to make a living. Some of them, presumably, had been fisherman or at least had some experience fishing, before immigrating to America. They fished for cod, mackerel, herring, halibut, hake, bass, and sturgeon. It was not an industry that involved the use of slaves.

A natural fit alongside fishing was shipbuilding. Again, presuming a previous skill set before immigrating, a number of people found that shipbuilding provided boats and ships necessary for the local fishing and shipping enterprise, but with lumber readily available and skilled workmen in the area, New England developed a shipbuilding industry that supplied ships to Europe as well. By 1750, there were 125 shipbuilders in the New England area. And since it involved skilled labor, it was not something that depended on the unskilled labor force of slaves.

66

Another early enterprise that was of a completely different nature (than fishing and shipbuilding) was the fur trade. Because of the market for fur in Europe (hats, stoles, coats, and other fashion accessories) the fur industry became one of the key features of the early American economy. Indeed, John Astor amassed a huge fortune dealing in furs. In the earliest days of the fur trade in North America (the 1500s), Europeans traded for furs with Native Americans. Later as immigration to North America increased, French Canadians and "mountain men" (who were neither French nor Canadian) did most of the trapping. There were no slaves involved.

So what is the point? The point is that in the early days of American economic activity, even before the United States formally existed, there was a great deal of economic activity that had nothing to do with slave labor. And that continued to be the case even when cotton exports, which did depend on slave labor, became for a time our number one export. Just because something is our country's number one export does not mean it is the foundation of our entire economy. For instance, according to Daniel Workman, in an article in *World's Top Exports*, in 2019, America's top export is machinery, bringing in a whopping $213.1 billion annually. This is 12.8% of our total exports. The rest of America's top ten exports includes:

Mineral fuels including oil: $189.9 billion
Electrical machinery, equipment: $176.3 billion
Aircraft, spacecraft: $139.1 billion
Vehicles: $130.6 billion
Optical, technical, medical apparatus: $89.6 billion

Plastics, plastic articles: $66.5 billion
Gems, precious metals: $63.8 billion
Pharmaceuticals: $48.4 billion
Organic chemicals: $40.2 billion

It's quite a varied list, isn't it? The thing to note is that the leading export makes up only 12.8% of the total of American exports. If someone argued that machinery, including computers, is that upon which the American economy is built, they would be mistaken. First, there is more to our economy than the products that we export. Second, the one at the top of the list, even though it is at the top, is simply not the feature upon which the entire American economy is built. Yet Marxist influenced scholars of various disciplines make this same basic argument in relation to cotton exports in the mid-1800s, claiming that America's economy was built on the backs of the slaves. They are mistaken—whether intentionally or unintentionally, I do not know. But I do know they are mistaken. I hope it is an honest mistake.

But just in case some are not yet convinced, let us go even deeper into the issue.

A Transportation Network
In an old but still very useful book entitled, *The Government and the Economy 1783-1861*, Columbia University Professor of Economics, Carter Goodrich, notes that: "Of all activities of American governments during the period, those most closely and deliberately intended to promote economic development were the efforts to improve the facilities of transportation" (Goodrich 1967:3).

Goodrich's book is a collection of original source documents from the years between 1783 and 1861 that show how the government proposed to stimulate economic growth. His contributions to the presentation of the original material are basically explanatory, helping the reader understand the context and intent of the original documents. It is an interesting presentation. His point in the quote above is that early on the government understood that if the American economy was going to grow and thrive, attention needed to be given to the transportation of goods. For instance, trappers worked in remote areas. How were they to get their pelts from those remote regions to locations where they could be sold, or to a harbor where they could be shipped to Europe? Means of viable transport for goods of all sorts were essential. So the government set out to encourage the development of transport methods.

What would these transport methods have been? In the early days they were roads and canals (manmade waterways), and railway transport. Most of the canals during those early years of development were in the northeast, between the Great Lakes and the Hudson River. There were not a lot of slaves in that region. In canals built further south, in Virginia, for instance, slave labor was utilized. But not so much in the more northern locations.

Though the federal government officially encouraged the construction of a suitable infrastructure, they did not always fund local building projects (the Erie Canal, for instance, was a New York State funded project). Roads were often the result of local governments or communities. In the South, one can easily imagine slaves being used to some extent in the construction of roads, bridges, canals, and so forth. But not in the regions where slaves were not part of the local culture. In the North and Western regions, few slaves were to be found. Infrastructure work was done by local people—white people, not black people. There were no slaves around to do the work.

But what has infrastructure got to do with the economy? Economic activity has to do with the production and distribution of goods. Those goods must be transported from where they originated to where they are utilized. Without channels of transportation, there can be no distribution; and without distribution, there can be no economic activity—no economy. One of the most basic features of any economy is the ability to transport goods, and the development of America's transportation infrastructure did not depend, except perhaps in a few local areas in the South, on slave labor. The American economy was not built on the backs of slaves.

Other Significant Features of the Early American Economy

Consider other features of the American economy. For many years, whale oil was used for burning in lamps. With the discovery of oil and how to refine it, kerosene became the preferred fuel for lamps. Slaves were not utilized in oil fields or refineries.

What about railroad work? The railroad played an enormous part in the economic development of America. The first American railroad was the Baltimore and Ohio, established in 1828. The next 75 years saw a great deal of track laid, so rail transportation was possible. Again, in the Southern states, slave labor may have been used. But not in

70

other regions. The railroads hired people. In many places, especially in the west, Chinese immigrants were hired to lay the track. The American rail system was not built by slaves.

What about the food industry in America—produce and meat? Family farms large and small generated the meat and produce consumed across the country. In some cases, a family farm might produce just enough to feed and support the family. But in other cases, surplus produce and meat were sold in local markets or shipped to major population centers. Other than on Southern plantations, this nationwide process of food production did not depend at all on slave labor. Small family farms produced most of the food consumed in America.

What about the lumber industry? As the nation grew, lumber was needed to build houses, barns, schools, churches, shops, train depots, warehouses, wagons, and more. Slaves were not involved in the logging industry.

Mining played a major role in the development of the American economy. Almost immediately after arriving in America, people discovered a wide variety of valuable ores: silver, copper, iron, and more. Eventually, mining enterprises were established, and ore was shipped to Europe or processed and used here in this country. Slave labor was not a major consideration in the mining enterprise of early America.

The California gold rush is an excellent example. When gold was discovered in California, it is estimated that eventually 300,000 people poured into the state. Many of them were mining gold; many were not. Instead, they provided goods and services to those who were. The population boom in the gold rush days of California impacted not only California, but the entire country. People were going to California, mining, investing, building, buying. Schools, houses, churches, stores, and other buildings went up. People needed clothes, tools, food. Much of what was needed had to be shipped in from other regions. Lots of people in the country enjoyed increased business opportunities because gold was found in California. Slave labor was not utilized in the economic expansion that grew out of the California gold rush.

Other features that impacted the development of the American economy were the industrialization and technological innovation made possible by the free enterprise and capitalistic spirit that characterized America. What were some of those things?

The steam engine
Steamboats
The tin can
Matches
The electromagnet
The typewriter
The sewing machine
The telegraph
The bicycle
The grain elevator
The process of pasteurization
Dynamite
The machine gun
The telephone
The light bulb

On and on the list could go, but this is sufficient to make the point: part of what made the U.S. economy so powerful and effective was industrialization and technological innovation—neither of which involved slave labor.

Two excellent sources for understanding how the U.S. economy evolved to become one of if not the most powerful and influential economy in history, include Bhu Srinivasan's book *Americana*, and the History Channel's series, *The Men Who Built America*. These are excellent sources that provide an overview of the kinds of things (economically speaking) that made America what it is.

While it is important to acknowledge the contribution the slaves made in the development of America, it is just as important to be accurate in the information provided and the conclusion drawn. Slavery was a fact in America as it was in every other culture both ancient and modern. It should not have happened, but it did. The slaves worked hard and made a great deal of money for their owners. There is no question about that. But was the American economy built on the backs of slaves? No, it was not. The American economy was much bigger than the segment of Southern agricultural that involved the use of slave labor. Slave labor was one feature (how large and significant is arguable) of a massive, multifaceted American economy, an economy so large and varied that it is impossible to select one single thing and claim that the entire economy was built on that feature. Those who claim that the entire American economy was built on a single feature of that economy simply do not know what they are talking about.

Summary

Was the United States economy built on the backs of slaves? No, it wasn't. Those who loudly proclaim that it was often cite the fact that for a few years in the mid-1800s cotton was America's number one export. That is true. However, that does not add up to cotton being the foundation of the entire American economy. There were many important economic enterprises that were part of the early American culture—fishing, shipbuilding, and fur trapping were three of them. Slave labor was not a factor in those enterprises. This was also the case in a number of other economic activities, such as developing an effective infrastructure (roads, canals, railroads) so that goods could be distributed. Without the distribution of goods, there is no economy.

With the development of a transportation infrastructure (which did not involve slave labor in any significant way—and in most cases not at all) a number of additional economic enterprises were able to thrive: mining, milling, the production of clothing, and tools, lumber, building, oil drilling and refining, food production, and many other things that did not in any way involve slave labor.

Two other important components of the 19th century American economy were industrialization and technological innovation. The list of important things that were developed in the 1800s is impressive. All these things were part of a massive, growing, thriving, economy that was not dependent in any way on slave labor.

All of this is not to say that the slaves made no significant contribution to the segment of the economy that was rooted in the Southern plantation system. They did. The work they did was hard and important. They made a lot of money for a few people. But the U.S. economy was not built on their backs. Those who say these things are simply wrong. One can only hope their mistake is due to ignorance rather than a deliberate attempt to mislead.

Chapter 7
An Unfortunate Reality ... Slavery Still Exists

According to statistics available online, somewhere between 25 and 40 million people live today in some form of slavery. Can this possibly be true? Yes. However, whether the number is 25 million or 40 million depends on how you define slavery. And the way most people who write about modern-day slavery define the term is a problem. Still, even if the number is 25 million instead of 40 million, that is a lot of people being held in some form of slavery, and is completely unacceptable. It is immoral and must be stopped.

A closer look at terms and definitions may shed some light on the estimated numbers.

Numbers and Definitions

First, let's deal with the numbers. Are there 25 million people living as slaves today, or 40 million? Since slavery, the way most people understand the term, is illegal virtually everywhere, all activity involving modern-day slavery takes place in an underground or *hidden in the shadows* sort of way. It is the dark secret that no one talks about. It is, therefore, impossible to gather accurate data about what's going on and to what degree. So the numbers are estimates. However, they are probably pretty good estimates. Somewhere between 25 and 40 million people live in slave-like conditions in the 21st century.

More problematic than gathering accurate data is defining what we are talking about. How is modern-day slavery to be defined? When most people think of slavery, they think of the kind of slavery we have discussed in previous chapters in this book: someone captured in battle or bought at a slave market, considered the property of his or her new owner, doing whatever they are ordered by their new master. But modern-day slavery does not look exactly like the slavery of years gone by.

Modern-day slavery usually takes one of the forms listed below.

Domestic servitude: a household "employee" (nanny, housekeeper, and so forth) who cannot leave her employment if she chooses—usually because she owes a debt to someone who brought her to this country, and the debt is being worked off. (This is also called bonded labor).

Forced labor: persons who, for various reasons cannot choose to leave the job they are doing. They are often forced to work for no pay under the threat of violence.

Child labor: any situation where a child is forced to work in some capacity.

Sex trafficking: involves women, men and children being held against their will and forced (by threat of violence or other form of coercion) to engage in commercial sex acts.

Bonded labor: being forced to work to pay off a debt. This is the most common form of modern-day slavery.

Forced marriage: a woman or girl forced to marry without her consent.

This particular list can be found on the site called: *End Slavery Now*. You can find many other lists that are virtually the same.

One of my complaints with this list (and others like it) is the inclusion of what they refer to as *forced* marriage. What they are actually referring to most of the time is *arranged* marriage, an old and respected cultural tradition. A number of sites that mention forced marriage do explain that this practice is linked to culture, but then disregard the social norms of those cultures that still practice arranged marriages, and condemn the practice as enslavement. This is misleading.

I can only assume from this misleading language and the blatant disregard for the sanctity of cultural heritage, that the people defining this practice as slavery have no training in cultural anthropology, and are completely lacking in cross-cultural sensitivity. The fact is that arranged marriages have been the cultural norm in virtually all cultures, including our Western culture, since the idea of marriage came into existence many thousands of years ago.

Until just recently in the West, parents (or families in general) have always decided who their sons and daughters will marry. Allowing inexperienced young people to decide who they will marry is a relatively new Western practice that has only been a social norm here in the West for 150 or 200 years. When compared to many thousands of years of arranged marriages, a couple of hundred years of choosing one's own spouse is a new custom. Parents from cultures where they still arrange marriages would say that allowing inexperienced young people to select their own marriage partner is the epitome of foolishness.

The idea that a son or daughter would willingly participate in an arranged marriage, marrying whomever he or she was told to marry, was simply a cultural given. It was the way things were done—and still is the way things are done in some cultures. One does what one has to do for the good of family. In those cultures, it is one's duty to assist in the creation of a new family alliance. That's the way things are done. And the marriages that came of those arranged unions are not considered demeaning or ugly in any way. And they certainly are not considered any form of slavery.

A few years ago, in one of my World Religion classes, I had a woman in class who was from a Middle Eastern culture where arranged marriages are still practiced. Her parents had arranged her marriage to her husband. She explained that she had only met him a couple of times before the wedding ceremony, but her father knew best, and it was her duty to marry him. So she did. In time, she said, she came to love her husband. He is a good husband, and they are happy together. The other students in the class, male and female, were shocked to hear this. I explained to them that that was the way all marriages had worked until just recently in the West.

Arranged marriages, therefore, were and remain an appropriate cultural construction. Slavery, though culturally accepted for thousands of years, was never appropriate because it was demeaning and dehumanizing, not recognizing the slave's humanity. Slavery was wrong because it denied a person the status of human, a status each human deserves. Arranged marriages, however, *are* appropriate (if a culture chooses to engage in the practice) because the practice allows sons and daughters to participate in the forming of family alliances, which suggests their considerable importance and value in the well-being of the family.

Part of the problem with the arranged marriage being called slavery is that the definition of slave-like conditions includes the woman not being able to leave the relationship if she desires. The problem there is that many of the countries where arranged marriages occur are very traditional cultures where a patriarchal social hierarchy still exists. This means that women are not considered equal, and that men have the final say in most matters. If a husband is not willing to grant his wife her "freedom," (that is grant her a divorce) there is nothing she can do about it. By our current Western standards, this seems horribly unfair, even immoral. However, this was the way things were in most cultures of the world until just a few hundred years ago. To identify the social structure of patriarchy with slavery (saying that patriarchy results in slavery) is not only entirely unwarranted, it's just plain silly. The rest of the world cannot be judged by modern Western standards. They have a right to their own cultural practices—to a degree. Nothing is completely open-ended. But just because a woman can't get a divorce if she wants one does not make her a slave. The idea is ridiculous.

So here's the question: why is a practice as old as marriage itself, a practice that was the cultural norm in all societies until just recently, a practice that is beneficial to the families of the bride and groom, suddenly condemned as unacceptable and labeled as slavery? Because the people writing about slavery today are apparently both unaware of the role of arranged marriages in history, and are sociocentric enough to accuse cultures different from our contemporary Western culture of wrongdoing simply because they dare to be different in an area where conformity to Western standards is demanded.

I realize that comment sounds rather harsh, but so does the charge of slavery. Just because a society practices arranged marriages does not mean that the parents who arrange the marriage of their daughter are selling or forcing her into slavery. That is an absurd charge rooted in Western sociocentric ignorance and arrogance, and is likely the result of very radical feminism.

Perhaps, someone may say, but what about child brides—as young as nine years old? It is true that some cultures where arranged marriages are the cultural norm do arrange marriages for young girls. However, what the critics of this practice do not tell you is that while there is a wedding ceremony, the marriage is not consummated until after the girl has gone through puberty. The man is not having sex with a prepubescent girl.

Someone may complain that such a young woman, even if she has gone through puberty, is still too young to be married. Well, actually that depends on the girl. Some girls are much more mature than others. When I was still teaching, I would raise the question of when someone is capable of making an informed decision about whether or not to engage in sex. In every class I asked, both men and women said they knew 14-year-old girls who were perfectly capable of making an informed decision regarding sexual activity. As a social scientist, I understand that that sort of informal questioning does not generate scientifically accurate data. However, it does give one a sense of what is going on in society, and apparently some girls are mature enough to decide about sex at a young age.

Generally speaking, though, in our culture we have extended childhood until well into the twenties. Even though one is legally an adult at age 21, few young people are fully mature adults at 21, ready to make adult decisions. A hundred years ago, however, things were quite different. In the late 1800s it was not uncommon for girls to marry at 14 or 15 years of age. My own grandmother, who was born in the 1890s, married my grandfather when she 12 years old. My grandfather was 13. They began their family, and my mother, born in 1914, was the second of nine children.

As time passed, the age when marriage was considered appropriate slowly crept up. Today, we typically think the mid to late twenties is an appropriate age for marriage. But just a hundred or so years ago in our own culture things were quite different.

The people who count women and girls who participate in arranged marriages as modern-day slaves are not taking into consideration cultural norms. They are using our current cultural standard regarding the rights of women as the standard by which all other cultures are to be judged. That sort of socio-centrism (being so focused in one's own social perspective that you cannot see the legitimacy of other social systems) is rooted in ignorance and arrogance. Personally, I would not want to live in a culture where arranged marriages were the social norm. But that does not mean that the system of arranged marriages is invalid and is tantamount to slavery. Women in arranged marriages, regardless of their age, are not slaves in any of the ways we normally understand the word slave.

Having said that, it is appropriate to note that all sorts of depravity occurs in every part of the world, and it is not unlikely that some women and young girls are actually forced to marry and then live in extremely restrictive and oppressive circumstances. Does that make them slaves? Are there 15 million of them out there? Unless you declare every woman in an arranged marriage as a slave, I suspect there are not. Most of what are referred to as forced marriages are simply arranged marriages.

But there is yet another concern in how many people are held in modern-day slavery. Another category of modern-day slavery is prisoners who are forced to work. Not every list includes prisoners who are required to work as slaves, but some do. The question is, regardless of what list the category appears on, is it in any way appropriate to refer to prisoners who are required to work as slaves? I think the answer is no, it is not. If someone is a rightly convicted criminal, that is, they were in fact guilty and are in prison as punishment for breaking the law, why is it treating them as a slave if they are required to work? Why is it dehumanizing to require convicted criminals to work? I have to work. Most everybody else has to work. Why is having to work dehumanizing? If work itself is not dehumanizing (and it is not), what is it about the process that makes it unacceptable for convicted criminals to have to work? What is it that makes a prisoner a slave? Is it that they are not given a choice as to the kind of work they do? When I was a kid in school there were quite a few things about which I had no choice. Did that make me a slave? Why should prisoners be fed, housed, clothed, given medical care, and so forth, and not be required to contribute in some way to the cost of those things? What is it about a prisoner having to work that makes them slaves? Nothing. The idea is silly.

So what is the point of all this? The point is that the people who write about modern-day slavery have, apparently, gotten carried away with the idea and gone off the rails. They are identifying things as slavery that clearly are not slavery. Therefore, we need to modify the numbers somewhat.

The current estimates that there are between 25 and 40 million modern-day slaves in world is probably on the high side. Since prisoners who are required to work are not slaves, and since most *forced* marriages are simply culturally appropriate *arranged* marriages and do not amount to slavery, we need to drop the artificially high number down a bit. Since it is estimated that there approximately 15 million women in *forced* marriages, we can toss out that number. Why? Because an arranged marriage, which is what most "forced" marriages are, is not slavery. If we take the 15 million out of the count, we are left with 25 million modern-day slaves. I am not aware of estimates about how many prisoners are required to work, so there is nothing to work with there. So if we take the 40 million number and subtract the 15 million of the so called forced marriages, we are left with 25 million modern-day slaves—which is a huge number and is completely unacceptable. Something must be done.

Where is this Happening
Using the categories of domestic servitude, forced labor (not including prisoners), child labor, sex trafficking,

and bonded labor, modern-day slavery can be identified in over 130 countries today. Bonded labor (someone who is working off a debt), sex trafficking, and forced labor are the largest categories of the kinds of slavery that exist today.

According to an article in *World Facts*, the top ten countries where slavery exists today include:

North Korea: The government forces millions of people to do jobs they would not choose to do. In North Korea, there are 104.6 people out of every 1,000 who live in slave-like conditions.
Eritera (Africa): The slave rate there is 93 out of 1,000
Burundi (Africa): 40 out of every 1,000 people live in slave-like conditions
Central African Republic: The rate of slavery there is 22.3 per 1,000
Afghanistan: 22.2 per 1,000
Mauritania (northwest Africa): 21.4 per 1,000
South Sudan (Africa): 20.5 per 1,000
Pakistan: 16.8 per 1,000
Cambodia: 16.8 per 1,000
Iran: 16.2 per 1,000

But lest we think modern-day slavery is only in far away places, the Global Slavery Index says there are over 400,000 people living in slave-like conditions right here in America. Most of them are illegal immigrants who find themselves working in some form of bonded labor, having paid someone to bring them into the country. They are working off the debt. But the debt repayment plan is structured so that the debt, based on a very low rate of wages, will never be paid off.

What is to be Done About Modern-day Slavery

Evil people who do not care how much suffering they cause exist everywhere in the world. They will do anything and hurt anyone just to put money in their pocket. And there's a lot of money involved. Modern-day slavery generates an estimated $150,000 billion each year. A lot of money is being made. Whenever there's a lot of money involved, the people making the money are very serious about hanging on to it. They aren't going to simply give up their source of income because someone says *"That's bad. You should stop."* So how do we stop them? The only way they can be stopped is for world governments to get serious about the problem.

Other than shining a light on the problems, agencies like the ones who post statistics online about modern-day slavery can do nothing about the problem. Sending them money is a waste of your money. Those agencies have no power to arrest and prosecute the offenders. Therefore, in the end, they are powerless. The only people who can address the issue in a meaningful way is the government. Only law enforcement agencies have the power to infiltrate the human trafficking rings and arrest the people involved.

The problem is they are not properly motivated. They know the problem exists. They put laws against it on the books. But then they sit back and do nothing to stop it. The only way to solve the problem of human trafficking and modern-day slavery is for concerned citizens to contact their government representatives and demand that they do more than they are presently doing. If you want to stop modern-day slavery, you need to require the government to get involved. You need to make them do their job. Sending money to agencies that advertise online will do nothing. Don't waste your money. Write your congressional representative and demand action.

Summary

Slavery is not a thing of the past. It still exists in various forms. Estimates (though questionable) are that as many as 40 million people live in slave-like conditions. What does that mean? The kind of slavery that existed in the past, people taken captives in battle or bought from a slave market, probably no longer exists. But people are transported and forced to engage in commercial sex acts or do other forms of forced labor, often because of a debt they incurred in an attempt to migrate to another country. Slavery today involves domestic servitude, forced labor of various kinds, child labor (often in factories), and sex trafficking.

Why would the 40 million number be questionable? Because it includes women in arranged marriages. The folks who research modern-day slavery refer to arranged marriages as *forced* marriages, and claim that the women involved are slaves. While there may be a few instances where extreme abuse is involved, most of the marriages they are describing are simply marriages in cultures where they still practice arranged marriages—just as we did here in the West until just a couple hundred years ago. Just because Western radical feminists don't like the idea of arranged marriages does not mean those marriages involve slavery. If you subtract the number of women involved in arranged

87

marriages (because they are not slaves) from the 40 million estimate, the actual number of modern-day slaves is probably about 25 million—still an enormous number and completely unacceptable.

The problem of modern-day slavery is not a *far away in another place* kind of a problem. There are over 400,000 slaves right here in the U.S. Something must be done. The only way to solve the problem is for world governments to hunt down and arrest and prosecute those who are getting rich in the modern-day slave business.

Chapter 8
Given the History of World Slavery,
What is the Proper Response

Slavery has existed from the earliest days of human interaction. Early on, people captured in battle became slaves to their captors. Later, slave markets were developed so the excess numbers of slaves could be sold at a profit.

In ancient times, slavery had nothing to do with race or ethnicity. Most of the time, slaves were of the same race as their masters. If slavery had nothing to do with race, what was it about? Power and economics. The stronger oppressed and enslaved the weaker and profited from the process.

If you study world history closely, one of the things you will notice is that strength and power tend to vacillate back and forth between different groups of people at different times. The people who are powerful and strong, who oppress and enslave, might themselves, a hundred or two hundred years later, be oppressed and enslaved. Over the 10,000 years or more of different groups of people oppressing and enslaving each other, just about every group of people out there was at one time slaves holders and at another time slaves. It is quite possible that at one time my ancestors enslaved yours or that your ancestors enslaved mine. Here is the crucial question—*What has that got to do with you and me?* As far as I can tell, not a single thing. So what that your ancestors, at some time in the past, enslaved my ancestors? So what that my ancestors, at some time in the past, enslaved yours? What does that have to do with how you and I interact? Nothing.

But there are people in our society who want to play up the fact that their ancestors were slaves. They want to use it to get special treatment. But since just about every group of people have, at some time, been enslaved by another group, why should any group who was enslaved get special treatment because of it? Some of my ancestors were, at some point, probably enslaved. Should I get special treatment? Some of your ancestors were, at some time, probably enslaved. Should you get special treatment? If everyone whose ancestors were enslaved somewhere along the way gets special treatment, then just about everyone is going to be getting special treatment. Frankly, it seems like a silly idea.

Slavery should never have happened. But it did. And it happened to just about every group of people that ever existed. Everyone has slavery in their past. Everyone is from a group of people who at one time owned slaves and at another time were slaves. How should we deal with that reality?

Acknowledge it and Make Sure it Never Happens Again

Pretending slavery never happened or forgetting that it did are not healthy ways of dealing with it. The only response to slavery that makes any sense is to acknowledge it, to understand that it was a part of human history that virtually all groups of people participated in. Everyone's ancestors were, at some time probably slave holders, and at some other time probably slaves. That's what happened. We need to acknowledge it. Everyone. African Americans need to acknowledge that African people also engaged in slavery. Most of the African slaves who ended up in America were captured by other Africans and sold to the Europeans who brought them here. Slavery wasn't a white sin, or a brown sin, or a black sin; it was a human sin. So we need to acknowledge it. Then we need to stop harping on it. Griping about what happened to our ancestors isn't going to make life better. It shouldn't have happened. It did happen. But it didn't happen to you, it happened to your ancestors. Get over it.

How people deal with past failures is important. Constantly talking about past failures is not helpful. Blaming someone for them isn't helpful. Whining about them isn't helpful. Acknowledge it, put it aside, and then do your best to be sure it never happens again. That's the key. It happened. But it can never be allowed to happen again.

What About Paying Reparations

Given that as I write this it is the beginning of the 2020 Presidential campaign season, one would expect to hear talk of reparations in regard to slavery. Paying slavery reparations is the idea that white Americans ought to pay black Americans for the damages done to their ancestral family in bringing their ancestors to America as slaves. The purchasing of slaves was such a horrible thing, the argument goes, that the descendants of the slaves ought to be compensated for what white people did to their ancestors.

There are several problems with the logic involved in the reparations argument. First, people of African origin were not the only people to be enslaved. Europeans, Asians, Native Americans, and Mesoamericans, were also enslaved—and by their own people, just as Africans were. So if people of African origin deserved to be paid reparations, so do every other people whose ancestors were enslaved. If everybody whose ancestors were enslaved got paid reparations from everyone who enslaved them, then everyone would be paying everyone else because all people groups engaged in slavery at some point. Just about everyone has an ancestor who held slaves, and just about everyone has an ancestor who was a slave. So everybody's got to pay everybody else! One popular political commentator, who happens to be black, looking at it from a different perspective asked: "Why do people who never owned slaves owe money to people who were never slaves?" The whole idea of reparations is silly.

The second flaw with the reparations proposal is that at this point in time, lots of African originated people have ancestors that reproduced with Europeans, which means they are of mixed race, part white, part black. Who owes whom the money? Take President Obama as an example. His father was a black African, his mother was a white woman. Does President Obama owe reparations, or should he receive reparations? Should his black half receive half the amount due from his white half? Or does his white half have to pay half of the reparations due to another black person? And what about the Africans who captured other Africans to sell to the European slave traders? Most of the Africans who were brought to America were sold to the Europeans by other Africans. Do the Africans who captured and sold Africans to Europeans owe reparations to the families of the Africans they captured and sold to the Europeans? Which Africans owe money to which African Americans? How could something like that possibly be sorted out? Again, the whole idea is simply silly.

Third, the reparations proposal is flawed because it is rooted in either ignorance or a lie. The people promising reparations (*If I am elected I will send a bill before congress ...*) are usually career politicians who know good and well that a reparations bill, even if one ever got submitted, would never pass the house and the senate and be signed by the president and become law so that checks could be written. They know that such a thing will NEVER happen. Yet they say they will push for it. When a person says she will try to do something, but know she will not or cannot do it, she is lying. Politicians who support reparations are lying. They are simply trying to buy the votes of people who want free stuff and who want to use the enslavement of their ancestors as an excuse for their own personal failures.

The only other reason someone would propose reparations is ignorance. They simply do not know the history of world slavery—that all people groups participated in slavery, that at some point in time every people group was both slave holder and slave. If they knew the history of slavery (as you now do), they would know that there is no single party guilty of the sin of slavery who should be held responsible and made to pay.

The idea of reparations is foolish. No one owes anyone anything.

It is a shame that slavery ever happened. But it did. Whining about it isn't going to change things. Using it as an excuse for one's own personal failures isn't going to make life better. It's time to lay the whole ugly event aside and get on with life. We need to make sure it never happens again, but constantly talking about it isn't going to accomplish anything useful.

And as far as modern-day slavery goes, everyone needs to demand that law enforcement does something about it. It is preventable only if we will require government to prevent it.

Summary

In each of the past couple of presidential campaigns someone trots out the idea of paying reparations to African Americans because their ancestors were slaves. It is simply a dishonest attempt to buy votes. Every politician who proposes the idea knows it could never become law so that checks could be written. And because they know that, when they say they are for reparations, they are lying.

There are serious problems with the idea of reparations to Africans Americans. One is that it is not only Africans who were enslaved. People from all people groups, at some time or another, were slaves. Also, people from all people groups were, at one time or another, slave holders. So who owes money to whom? Second, since some people are a mix of black and white, who pays whom? Does the white half pay the black half? And what about the black Africans who captured other black Africans to sell to the European slave traders? Do they owe money to someone? You would think so.

The whole idea of reparations is silly. Everybody who ever had an ancestor who ever owned a slave would owe someone money. But since all people groups at some point in time owned slaves, everybody would owe everybody money. The idea is ridiculous.

Conclusion

From at least the time people began living together in settled villages, slavery became part of human society. It never should have, but it did. All ancient peoples captured other ancient people in battle, people of the same race, especially the women and children, and kept them as slaves.

Every ancient society kept slaves: Sumer, Babylon, Egypt, Israel, Greece, Rome, and many others. There was slavery in the Dark Ages after the fall of Rome, slavery in the Middle Ages, and slavery in the Modern period. Why? Because people have free will and can choose how to behave. They were also childish and narcissistic, caring only about themselves. They refused to consider what being human meant and refused to consider all people as equals and worthy of respect. When people don't care about other people, all kinds of ugly things will happen.

But surely the African slave trade was worse than all the slavery that went before. Why would anyone think so? When you are a possession and can be treated any way your owner likes, your life is miserable. Whether you work in a copper mine or a cotton field, when you can be beaten or sold on the whim of your master, life is miserable. I have heard some African Americans claim that the African slavery was worse than any previous slavery. On what evidence would they base that claim? None. There is no evidence that the Atlantic passage slavery was any worse than slavery in ancient Rome or anywhere else. Given that ancient Assyria was one of the most brutal societies in history, I suspect if you could identify the worst slavery ever, it would be the slavery that existed in ancient Assyria, for the Assyrians are considered the cruelest, most ruthless people in history.

The Atlantic passage slave trade was awful for the slaves and profitable for the Southern plantation owners who owned most of the slaves in America. As bad as life was for the slaves, life was pretty good for their masters. They got rich off the work of their slaves. Some have claimed that the American economy was built on the backs of the slaves. Is that true? You hear it quite often. No, it is not true. The American economy was not built on the backs of slaves. The slaves had a huge impact on the economy of the South. But the larger American economy was so diverse, so multifaceted, that there is no way the entire U.S. economy was built on the work of the slaves. The idea that the work of the slaves provided the foundation for the economy of the U.S. is argued by leftist, Marxist "scholars" who want to discredit the American capitalist system of free enterprise, crediting the slaves with that which was accomplished by American farmers and industrialists.

It would be nice if we could say that slavery has been eradicated from the world. But we can't say that because it hasn't been. Slavery still exists. It may not exist in the same form as it has in the past, but it still exists. It exists in the form of sex trafficking, child labor, bonded labor, and forced labor of various kinds.

Defining modern-day slavery can be challenging. Some are of the opinion that women in arranged marriages are slaves. That view is an extreme exaggeration and likely the result of radical feminism. An arranged marriage does not create a slave. But even without counting women in arranged marriages, there are probably 25 million modern-day slaves, over 400,000 of them right here in the United States. It is a serious problem that must be addressed. The only way to effectively address it is for government law enforcement agencies around the world to infiltrate and root out the slavers. Sending money to agencies that advertise online will do nothing to end slavery, so don't waste your money. A better course of action is to write your congressperson or senator, insisting that they make ending modern-day slavery a priority.

So what have we learned from our brief foray into the history of slavery? It happened. It shouldn't have, but it did. It happened everywhere, with all people groups being involved. At one point a particular group may have been weaker and were captured and made to serve as slaves of another stronger group (usually of the same race or ethnic group). But at another time, perhaps several hundred years later, the weaker group became strong, and they became the masters. At some point in time, some of your ancestors were probably slaves and at another they may have been the ones doing the enslaving. Europeans enslaved other Europeans, Africans enslaved other Africans, Native American tribes enslaved other Native American tribes, Mesoamerican tribes enslaved other Mesoamerican tribes, Asians enslaved other Asians. Over the ten or twelve thousand-year history of slavery, everyone was involved.

What are we to do with this information? We need to acknowledge that slavery occurred, and everyone engaged in the practice. Everyone believed it was just the way things worked. If you were strong, you oppressed and enslaved the weak. It shouldn't have happened, but it did. Some of your ancestors might have enslaved some of my ancestors. Some of mine might have enslaved some of yours. How should that impact how you and I interact with each other? It should not impact our interaction at all. What does it matter who did what to whom 200 or 2,000 or 10,000 years ago? Whining and complaining about what happened in ages gone by is a waste of time. It happened. It shouldn't have. Let it go and move on.

The idea of paying reparations to those whose ancestors were slaves is silly because if you go back far enough, at one time or another just about everyone's ancestors were slaves. The proposal that white people owe black people damages for what their ancestors suffered is an idea rooted in ignorance and dishonesty. The candidates who say they support paying reparations are either ignorant of the history of slavery, or are simply ignoring it so they can propose something that they believe will get them votes. In other words, they are trying to buy votes. Yet they know that a bill proposing the payment of reparation will never get passed in both the house and the senate and be signed into law by the president. It just isn't going to happen. And they know that. But they support it anyway. Which means they are lying. Shame on them. The idea of anyone paying reparations to anyone else because someone in the past enslaved someone else is just silly.

You can see all of Dr. Rogers book on his
Amazon Author's page at
authorcentral.amazon.com/gp/books

Works Cited

Adkins, Lesley and Roy A. Adkins
    1994 *Handbook to Life in Ancient Rome*. Oxford: Oxford University Press.

Beard, Mary
    2015 *SPQR A History of Ancient Rome*. New York: Liveright Publishing Corporation.

Camp, John and Elizabeth Fisher
    2002 *The World of the Ancient Greeks*. London: Thames and Hudson.

Cartledge, Paul
    2002 *Cambridge Illustrated History: Ancient Greece*. Editor, Paul Cartledge. Cambridge: Cambridge University Press.

Davenport, John
    2007 *The Age of Feudalism*. Detroit: Gale Cengage Learning.

Davis, Robert C.
    2003 *Christian Slaves, Muslims Masters: White Slavery in the Mediterranean, the   Barbary Coast, and Italy, 1500-1800*. New York: Palgrave McMillan.

End Slavery Now
    2019 *Slavery Today*.
    http://www.endslaverynow.org/learn/slavery-

today?gclid=EAIaIQobChMI8rj0g9GZ5AIVhIbACh
1-1QH7EAAYAyAAEgKVOPD_BwE

Freeman, Charles
1996 *Egypt, Greece, and Rome: Civilizations of the Ancient Mediterranean.* Oxford: Oxford University Press.

Global Slavery Index
2019 *United States.*
https://www.globalslaveryindex.org/2018/findings/country- studies/united-states/

Goodrich, Carter
1967 *The Government and the Economy 1783-1861.* Indianapolis: The Bobbs-Merrill Company.

History Channel, The
2012 *The Men Who Built America.* Executive Producer Stephen David, et al.

Karuga, James.
2019 *Slavery Today: Countries With the Highest Prevalence of Modern Slaves.* World Atlas. worldatlas.com/articles/countries-with-the-most-modern-slaves-today.html.

Kramer, Samuel Noah.
1963 *The Sumerians: Their History, Culture, and Character.* Chicago: University of   Chicago Press.

Leick, Gwendolyn
> 2003 *The Babylonians: An Introduction.* New York: Routledge.

Meltzer, Milton.
> 1993 *Slavery: A World History.* Da Capo Press.

Roberts, J.M.
> 2002 *Ancient History: From the First Civilizations to the Renaissance.* Editor J.M. Roberts.   London: Duncan Baird Publishers.

Rogers, Glenn
> 2018 *A Brief History of Capitalistic Free Enterprise, And Why it is Better than ANY Form of Socialism.* Abilene: Simpson & Brook, Publishers.

> 2018 *Proof of God: Inquiries Into the Philosophy of Religion, A Concise Introduction.*   Abilene: Simpson & Brook, Publishers.

Scheidel, Walter
> 2012 *The Cambridge Companion to the Roman Economy.* Editor, Walter Scheidel.   Cambridge: Cambridge University Press.

Srinivasan, Bhu
> 2017 *Americana.* New York: Penguin.

Thomas, Hugh
    1997 *The Slave Trade: The Story of the Atlantic Slave Trade 1440-1870*. New York: Simon   and Schuster Paperbacks.

Wilson, John
    1951 *The Culture of Ancient Egypt*. Chicago: University of Chicago Press.

Woolf, Greg
    2005 *Ancient Civilizations: The Illustrated Guide to Belief, Mythology, and Art*. Editor   Greg   Woolf. San Diego: Thunder Bay Press.

Workman, Daniel
    2019 *United States Top Ten Exports*. World's Top Exports.
    http://www.worldstopexports.com/united-states-top-10-exports/

CPSIA information can be obtained
at www.ICGtesting.com
Printed in the USA
LVHW041207170820
663375LV00003B/258

9 781732 488182